THE
Martini
A COLLECTION

Cat Sass Media Design
Nanaimo, British Columbia
Canada

THE
Martini
A COLLECTION

For Guy, who is always there. Without his support, his patience, his ideas and his love this book would not exist. For Josh and Haley who make the hard work worth it. For my Mom who makes the hard work easier. For Nola who defines the word friend.

I love you all!

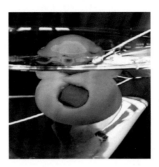

Disclaimer:

Printed and bound in Canada

Compiled by Liza Schafhauser & Guy Taylor

Photography: Terry Patterson, Nanaimo, BC

Layout and Design: Liza Schafhauser

The Martini, A Collection/Liza Schafhauser

www.cat-sassmedia.com

TABLE OF CONTENTS

In the beginning there was...

The Martinez
4 parts Gin
1 part Sweet Vermouth
2 dashes Maraschino Liqueur
1 dash Orange Bitters
2 small Ice Cubes

Circa 1862

Many believe today's Martini
evolved from this cocktail.

THE CLASSICS

"One martini is alright, two is too many,
three is not enough."

— James Thurber —

Absolutely Fabulous

1 part Gin
1 part Dry Vermouth
5 dashes Bitters

Pour ingredients into a shaker with cracked ice and shake. Strain into chilled martini glasses. Garnish with a lemon twist.

Allies Martini

3 parts Gin
2 parts Dry Vermouth
1 part Jägermeister

Pour ingredients into a shaker with cracked ice and shake well. Strain into chilled martini glasses. Garnish with a lemon twist.

Artillery Martini

3 parts Gin
1 part Sweet Vermouth

Pour ingredients into a shaker with cracked ice and shake well. Strain into chilled martini glasses. Garnish with a lemon twist.

Astoria Martini

3 parts Gin or Vodka
1 part Dry Vermouth
1 dash Bitters

Pour ingredients into a shaker with cracked ice and shake well. Strain into chilled martini glasses. Garnish with an orange twist.

Bennett

1 part Gin
5 dashes Bitters
1/2 tsp Bar Sugar

Pour ingredients into a shaker with cracked ice and shake well. Strain into chilled martini glasses. Garnish with a lemon twist.

Bone Dry Diablo Martini

4 parts Vodka
4 parts Gin
1 part Sweet White Vermouth
1 dash of Scotch

Pour Scotch into a chilled martini glass, swirl to coat inside. Pour ingredients into a shaker with cracked ice and shake well. Strain into prepared martini glasses. Garnish with an olive.

Boston Bullet

4 parts Gin or Vodka
1 part Dry Vermouth

Pour ingredients into a shaker with cracked ice and shake well. Strain into chilled martini glasses. Garnish with an almond stuffed olive.

Buckeye Martini

6 parts Gin
1 part Dry Vermouth

Pour ingredients into a shaker with cracked ice and shake well. Strain into chilled martini glasses. Garnish with a black olive.

Classic Martini

2 parts Gin
1 part Dry Vermouth
1 dash Bitters

Pour ingredients into a shaker with cracked ice and shake well. Strain into chilled martini glasses. Garnish with an olive.

Classic Vodka Martini

2 parts Vodka
1 part Dry Vermouth
1 dash Bitters

Pour ingredients into a shaker with cracked ice and shake well. Strain into chilled martini glasses. Garnish with an olive.

Colony Club Martini

6 parts Gin
1 part Pernod
5 dashes Bitters

Pour ingredients into a shaker with cracked ice and shake well. Strain into chilled martini glasses. Garnish with an orange twist.

Decal's Negroni

2 parts Gin
1 part Sweet Vermouth
4 parts Campari

Pour ingredients into a shaker with cracked ice and shake well. Strain into chilled martini glasses. Garnish with an orange twist.

Diplomat Martini

2 parts Dry Vermouth
1 part Sweet Vermouth

Pour ingredients into a shaker with cracked ice and shake well. Strain into chilled martini glasses. Garnish with a lemon twist and a cherry.

Dirty Martini

8 parts Gin
1 part Dry Vermouth
1 tsp Olive Juice

Pour ingredients into a shaker with cracked ice and shake well. Strain into chilled martini glasses. Garnish with an olive

Dirty Vodka Martini

8 parts Vodka
1 part Dry Vermouth
1 tsp Olive Juice

Pour ingredients into a shaker with cracked ice and shake well. Strain into chilled martini glasses. Garnish with an olive.

Dusty Martini

16 parts Vodka
1 part Scotch

Pour Scotch into a chilled martini glass, swirl to coat inside. Pour chilled vodka into prepared glass. Garnish with an olive.

Emerald Martini

12 parts Gin
4 parts Dry Vermouth
1 part Green Chartreuse

Pour ingredients into a shaker with cracked ice and shake well. Strain into chilled martini glasses. Garnish with a lemon twist.

Emerald Vodka Martini

12 parts Vodka
4 parts Dry Vermouth
1 part Green Chartreuse

Pour ingredients into a shaker with cracked ice and shake well. Strain into chilled martini glasses. Garnish with a lemon twist.

Extra Dry Lemon Vodka Martini

1 part Vodka
1/4 tsp Lemon Juice
3 to 5 drops Dry Vermouth

Pour ingredients into a shaker with cracked ice and shake well. Strain into chilled martini glasses. Garnish with a lemon twist.

Fare Thee Well Martini

6 parts Gin
1 part Dry Vermouth
1 dash Sweet Vermouth
1 dash Cointreau

Pour ingredients into a shaker with cracked ice and shake well. Strain into chilled martini glasses. Garnish with an orange twist

Farmer's Martini

6 parts Gin
1 part Dry Vermouth
1 part Sweet Vermouth
5 dashes Bitters

Pour ingredients into a shaker with cracked ice and shake well. Strain into chilled martini glasses. Garnish with a lemon twist.

Fifty-Fifty Martini

1 part Gin or Vodka
1 part Dry Vermouth

Pour ingredients into a shaker with cracked ice and shake well. Strain into chilled martini glasses. Garnish with a lemon twist.

Fino Martini

6 parts Gin or Vodka
1 part Fino Sherry

Pour ingredients into a shaker with cracked ice and shake well. Strain into chilled martini glasses. Garnish with a lemon twist.

Fisherman's Friend

2 parts Gin or Vodka
1 part Dry Vermouth

Pour ingredients into a shaker with cracked ice and shake well. Strain into chilled martini glasses. Garnish with an anchovy stuffed olive.

Frozen Martini

5 parts Frozen Gin
1 part Frozen Dry Vermouth

Pour ingredients into a shaker with cracked ice and shake well. Strain into chilled martini glasses. Garnish with two frozen almond stuffed olives.

Gibson

8 parts Gin
1 part Dry Vermouth

Pour ingredients into a shaker with cracked ice and shake well. Strain into chilled martini glasses. Garnish with an onion.

Gilroy Martini

3 parts Buffalo Grass Vodka
1 part Dry Vermouth
2 drops Garlic Juice

Pour ingredients into a shaker with cracked ice and shake well. Strain into chilled martini glasses. Garnish with a garlic stuffed olive.

Gimlet

7 parts Gin or Vodka
3 parts Lime Juice

Pour ingredients into a shaker with cracked ice and shake well. Strain into chilled martini glasses. Garnish with a lime twist.

Gin & It

4 parts Gin
1 part Sweet Vermouth

Pour ingredients into a shaker with cracked ice and shake well. Strain into chilled martini glasses. Garnish with a lemon twist.

Gin Martini

2 parts Gin
1 part Dry Vermouth

Pour ingredients into a shaker with cracked ice and shake well. Strain into chilled martini glasses. Garnish with an olive.

Gin Martini Dry

5 parts Gin
1 part Dry Vermouth

Pour ingredients into a shaker with cracked ice and shake well. Strain into chilled martini glasses. Garnish with an olive.

Gin Martini Extra Dry

8 parts Gin
1 part Dry Vermouth

Pour ingredients into a shaker with cracked ice and shake well. Strain into chilled martini glasses. Garnish with an olive.

Gin Martini Medium

3 parts Gin
1 part Dry Vermouth
1 part Sweet Vermouth

Pour ingredients into a shaker with cracked ice and shake well. Strain into chilled martini glasses. Garnish with an olive.

Gin Martini Sweet

1 part Gin
1 part Sweet Vermouth

Pour ingredients into a shaker with cracked ice and shake well. Strain into chilled martini glasses. Garnish with an olive.

Gin Salad

4 parts Gin
1 part Dry Vermouth

Pour ingredients into a shaker with cracked ice and shake well. Strain into chilled martini glasses. Garnish with 3 olives and 2 onions.

Ginitini

8 parts Gin
1 part Onion Juice

Pour ingredients into a shaker with cracked ice and shake well. Strain into chilled martini glasses. Garnish with an olive.

Golf Martini

4 parts Gin
1 part Dry Vermouth
5 dashes Bitters

Pour ingredients into a shaker with cracked ice and shake well. Strain into chilled martini glasses. Garnish with an olive.

Green Pearl Martini

8 parts Vodka
1 part Dry Vermouth

Pour ingredients into a shaker with cracked ice and shake well. Strain into chilled martini glasses. Garnish with an onion stuffed olive.

Gypsy Martini

4 parts Gin
1 part Sweet Vermouth

Pour ingredients into a shaker with cracked ice and shake well. Strain into chilled martini glasses. Garnish with a cherry.

Haschi Baschi Martini

2 parts Gin
1 part Campari

Pour ingredients into a shaker with cracked ice and shake well. Strain into chilled martini glasses. Garnish with a lemon twist.

Hasty Martini

8 parts Gin
2 parts Dry Vermouth
1 part Grenadine
5 dashes Pernod

Pour ingredients into a shaker with cracked ice and shake well. Strain into chilled martini glasses. Garnish with a cherry.

Hotel Plaza Martini

1 part Gin
1 part Dry Vermouth
1 part Sweet Vermouth

Pour ingredients into a shaker with cracked ice and shake well. Strain into chilled martini glasses. Garnish with a cherry.

Iceberg Martini

3 parts Vodka or Gin
1 frozen Dry Vermouth Cube

Pour Gin or Vodka into a shaker with cracked ice and shake well. Strain into chilled martini glasses. Garnish with the frozen cube of dry vermouth and an olive.

In & Out Martini

7 parts Vodka
1 part Dry Vermouth

Swirl Dry Vermouth around chilled martini glass and discard excess. Pour chilled vodka into prepared glass and garnish with two blue cheese stuffed olives and a lemon twist.

Knickerbocker Martini

6 parts Gin
2 parts Dry Vermouth
1 part Sweet Vermouth

Pour ingredients into a shaker with cracked ice and shake well. Strain into chilled martini glasses. Garnish with a lemon twist.

Knock Out Martini

2 parts Gin
1 part Pernod
1 part Dry Vermouth

Pour ingredients into a shaker with cracked ice and shake well. Strain into chilled martini glasses.

Kup's Indispensible

4 parts Gin
1 part Dry Vermouth
1 part Sweet Vermouth

Pour ingredients into a shaker with cracked ice and shake well. Strain into chilled martini glasses. Garnish with an orange twist.

Martunia

6 parts Gin
1 part Dry Vermouth
1 part Sweet Vermouth

Pour ingredients into a shaker with cracked ice and shake well. Strain into chilled martini glasses. Garnish with edible flowers.

Memories of Another Day

8 parts Vodka
6 parts Dry Vermouth
1 part Bitters

Pour ingredients into a shaker with cracked ice and shake well. Strain into chilled martini glasses. Garnish with an olive.

Mother-in-Law Cure

3 parts Gin
1 part Dry Vermouth

Place spiralled lemon rinds with an olive and two ice cubes into bottom of chilled martini glasses. Pour ingredients into a glass pitcher with ice and stir. Pour into prepared martini glasses.

Naked Martini

1 part Frozen Gin

Pour into chilled martini glasses. Garnish with an olive.

Negroni Martini

1 part Gin
1 part Sweet Vermouth
1 part Campari

Pour ingredients into a shaker with cracked ice and shake well. Strain into chilled martini glasses. Garnish with an orange slice.

Octopus' Garden

3 parts Gin
1 part Dry Vermouth

Pour ingredients into a shaker with cracked ice and shake well. Strain into chilled martini glasses. Garnish with a smoked baby octopus and a black olive.

Oyster Martini

6 parts Vodka
1 part Dry Vermouth

Pour ingredients into a shaker with cracked ice and shake well. Strain into chilled martini glasses. Garnish with a smoked oyster.

Paisley Martini

8 parts Gin
1 part Dry Vermouth
1 parts Scotch

Pour ingredients into a shaker with cracked ice and shake well. Strain into chilled martini glasses. Garnish with a lemon twist.

Perfect Martini

5 parts Vodka
2 parts Dry Vermouth
1 part Pernod

Pour ingredients into a shaker with cracked ice and shake well. Strain into chilled martini glasses. Garnish with a jumbo olive.

Pernod Martini

8 parts Gin
2 parts Dry Vermouth
1 part Pernod

Pour ingredients into a shaker with cracked ice and shake well. Strain into chilled martini glasses. Garnish with an onion stuffed olive.

Piccadilly Martini

6 parts Gin
2 parts Dry Vermouth
1 part Pernod
1 dash Grenadine

Pour ingredients into a shaker with cracked ice and shake well. Strain into chilled martini glasses. Garnish with a cherry.

Pink Gin Martini

1 part Gin
1 tsp Bitters

Pour ingredients into a shaker with cracked ice and shake well. Strain into chilled martini glasses. Garnish with a lemon twist.

Plaza Martini

1 part Gin
1 part Dry Vermouth
1 part Sweet Vermouth

Pour ingredients into a shaker with cracked ice and shake well. Strain into chilled martini glasses. Garnish with a lemon twist.

Racquet Club Martini

3 parts Gin
1 part Dry Vermouth
5 dashes Bitters

Pour ingredients into a shaker with cracked ice and shake well. Strain into chilled martini glasses. Garnish with a lemon twist.

Silver Bullet

1 part Gin
1 splash Scotch

Pour ingredients into a shaker with cracked ice and shake well.
Strain into chilled martini glasses.

Silver Fox

2 parts Vodka or Gin
1 part Dry Vermouth

Pour ingredients into a shaker with cracked ice and shake well.
Strain into chilled martini glasses. Garnish with flakes of silver leaf.

Smoky Martini

12 parts Gin
2 parts Dry Vermouth
1 part Scotch

Pour ingredients into a shaker with cracked ice and shake well.
Strain into chilled martini glasses. Garnish with a lemon twist.

Sweet Martini

3 parts Gin
1 part Sweet Vermouth
1 dash Bitters

Pour ingredients into a shaker with cracked ice and shake well.
Strain into chilled martini glasses. Garnish with an orange twist.

Sweetie Martini

6 parts Gin
1 part Dry Vermouth
1 part Sweet Vermouth

Pour ingredients into a shaker with cracked ice and shake well.
Strain into chilled martini glasses. Garnish with a lemon twist.

Third Degree Martini

6 parts Gin
2 parts Dry Vermouth
1 part Pernod

Pour ingredients into a shaker with cracked ice and shake well.
Strain into chilled martini glasses. Garnish with star anise.

Twenty Four Carrot Martini

8 parts Vodka
1 part Dry Vermouth

Pour ingredients into a shaker with cracked ice and shake well. Strain into chilled martini glasses. Garnish with a baby carrot.

Vesper Martini

6 parts Gin
2 parts Vodka
1 part Blond Lillet

Pour ingredients into a shaker with cracked ice and shake well. Strain into chilled martini glasses. Garnish with a jumbo olive.

Vodka Martini

2 parts Vodka
1 part Dry Vermouth

Pour ingredients into a shaker with cracked ice and shake well. Strain into chilled martini glasses. Garnish with an olive.

Vodka Martini Dry

5 parts Vodka
1 part Dry Vermouth

Pour ingredients into a shaker with cracked ice and shake well. Strain into chilled martini glasses. Garnish with an olive.

Vodka Martini Extra Dry

8 parts Vodka
1 part Dry Vermouth

Pour ingredients into a shaker with cracked ice and shake well. Strain into chilled martini glasses. Garnish with an olive.

Vodka Martini Medium

3 parts Vodka
1 part Dry Vermouth
1 part Sweet Vermouth

Pour ingredients into a shaker with cracked ice and shake well. Strain into chilled martini glasses. Garnish with an olive.

Vodka Martini Sweet

1 part Vodka
1 part Sweet Vermouth

Pour ingredients into a shaker with cracked ice and shake well. Strain into chilled martini glasses. Garnish with an olive.

Vodka Salad

4 parts Vodka
1 part Dry Vermouth

Pour ingredients into a shaker with cracked ice and shake well. Strain into chilled martini glasses. Garnish with 3 olives and 2 onions.

Wild Nights Dirty Gin Martini

4 parts Gin
1 part Extra Dry Vermouth
3 parts Olive Juice

Pour ingredients into a shaker with cracked ice and shake well. Strain into chilled martini glasses. Garnish with four olives.

"Work is the curse of
the drinking class"

— Oscar Wilde —

THE CELEBS

> "When I have one martini, I feel bigger, wiser, taller.
> When I have the second, I feel superlative.
> When I have more, there's no holding me."
> — William Faulkner —

Aphrodite's Love Potion

1 part Vodka
2 parts Fine Brandy
5 parts Pineapple Juice

Pour ingredients into a shaker with cracked ice and shake well. Strain into chilled martini glasses. Garnish with an orange slice and maraschino cherry.

Baby Face Martini

6 parts Strawberry Vodka
1 part Dry Vermouth
1 part Maraschino Liqueur

Pour ingredients into a shaker with cracked ice and shake well. Strain into chilled martini glasses. Garnish with a lemon twist.

Barney Martini

8 parts Vodka
4 parts Melon Liqueur
4 parts Blue Curaçao
1 part Crème de Cacao
1 part Margherita Mix

Pour ingredients into a shaker with cracked ice and shake well. Strain into chilled martini glasses. Garnish with a lemon twist and a lime wedge.

Barry M. Martini

3 parts Vodka
1 part Blue Curaçao Liqueur
2 parts Cranberry Juice
1 part Lime Juice

Pour ingredients into a shaker with cracked ice and shake well. Strain into chilled martini glasses. Garnish with a wedge of lemon.

Black Beard Martini

5 parts Vodka
4 parts Dark Crème de Cacao
1 part Black Currant Schnapps

Pour ingredients into a shaker with cracked ice and shake well. Strain into chilled martini glasses. Garnish with shaved white chocolate.

Black Dahlia Martini

6 parts Vodka
1 part Cinnamon Liqueur
1 part Raspberry Liqueur
Dark Chocolate Shavings

Pour ingredients except chocolate into a shaker with cracked ice and shake well. Strain into chilled martini glasses. Garnish with fresh raspberries and float chocolate shavings.

Cherry Cognac Jr. Martini

5 parts Vodka
1 part Cognac
1 part Cranberry Juice
1 squeeze of Lemon Juice
1 dash of Maraschino Liqueur

Pour ingredients into a shaker with cracked ice and shake well. Strain into chilled martini glasses. Garnish with a cognac marinated cherry.

Church Lady Martini

2 parts Gin
1 part Dry Vermouth
1 part Orange Juice

Pour ingredients into a shaker with cracked ice and shake well. Strain into chilled martini glasses. Garnish with a lemon, lime and orange slices.

Churchill's Martini

1 part Gin
Bottle of Dry Vermouth

Pour chilled Gin into chilled martini glasses. Look at the bottle of vermouth. Garnish with an olive.

Dean Martin Martini

1 part Lemon Vodka
1 part Vodka
1 dash Dry Vermouth

Add cracked ice to a low cocktail glass. Add vodkas, introduce a few dashes of vermouth. Swirl. Twist a bit of lemon and add the peel.

Delilah Martini

2 parts Gin
1 part Triple Sec
1 part Lemon Juice

Pour ingredients into a shaker with cracked ice and shake well.
Strain into chilled martini glasses. Garnish with a lemon twist.

El Presidente Martini

12 parts Vodka
4 parts Dry Vermouth
4 parts Triple Sec
4 parts Lemon Juice
1 part Grenadine

Pour ingredients except grenadine into a shaker with cracked ice
and shake well. Strain into chilled martini glasses. Add a few drops
of grenadine to each glass. Garnish with a lemon twist.

FDR's Martini

2 parts Gin
1 part Dry Vermouth
1 tsp Olive Brine

Pour ingredients into a shaker with cracked ice and shake well.
Strain into chilled martini glasses. Garnish with an olive.

Farmer's Daughter Martini

2 parts Vodka
1 part Goldschläger
3 parts Apple Juice

Pour ingredients into a shaker with cracked ice and shake well.
Strain into chilled martini glasses. Garnish with a slice of apple rind.

Gold Finger Martini

1 part Vodka
1 part Goldschläger

Pour ingredients into a chilled pitcher with cracked ice and stir. Pour
into chilled martini glasses. Garnish with a lemon twist.

Green Hornet

2 parts Gin
1 splash Dry Vermouth
2 splashes Green Tabasco Sauce

Pour ingredients into a shaker with cracked ice and shake well. Strain
into chilled martini glasses. Garnish with a jalapeno stuffed olive.

Green Hornet 2

4 parts Gin
1 part Dry Vermouth
1 splash Green Tabasco Sauce

Pour ingredients into a shaker with cracked ice and shake well. Strain into chilled martini glasses. Garnish with an olive.

Gumbee Martini

8 parts Vodka
1 part Green Crème De Menthe

Pour ingredients into a shaker with cracked ice and shake well. Strain into chilled martini glasses. Garnish with whipped cream and a kiwi slice.

Hemingway Martini

4 parts Vodka
4 parts White Rum
1 part Cherry Liqueur
3 parts Lime Juice
1 part Grapefruit Juice

Pour ingredients into a shaker with cracked ice and shake well. Strain into chilled martini glasses. Garnish with a lemon twist.

Hoffman House Martini

8 parts Gin
1 part Dry Vermouth
5 drops Bitters

Pour ingredients into a shaker with cracked ice and shake well. Strain into chilled martini glasses. Garnish with an olive.

Hoosier Martini

4 parts Buffalo Grass Vodka
2 parts Light Rum
1 part Dry Vermouth

Pour ingredients into a shaker with cracked ice and shake well. Strain into chilled martini glasses. Garnish with a lemon twist.

Jack London Martini

6 parts Currant Vodka
2 parts Dubonnet Blanc
1 part Maraschino Liqueur

Pour ingredients into a shaker with cracked ice and shake well. Strain into chilled martini glasses. Garnish with a lemon twist.

Jack Rose Martini

4 parts Vodka
4 parts Brandy
2 parts Lime Juice
1 part Grenadine

Pour ingredients except grenadine into a shaker with cracked ice and shake well. Strain into chilled martini glasses. Place a drop of grenadine in each glass. Garnish with a lime twist.

Jackie O Martini

6 parts Vodka
3 parts Pineapple Juice
1 part Apricot Brandy
1 dash Grenadine

Pour ingredients except grenadine into a shaker with cracked ice and shake well. Add a dash of grenadine to each glass. Strain mixture into chilled martini glasses. Garnish with a pineapple wedge.

Jacques Cousteau

6 parts Vodka
2 parts Blue Curaçao
1 part Ruby Red Grapefruit Juice

Pour ingredients into a shaker with cracked ice and shake well. Strain into chilled martini glasses. Garnish with a lemon twist and cranberries.

James Bond Martini

6 parts Gin
2 parts Vodka
1 part Lillet

Pour ingredients into a shaker with cracked ice and shake well. Strain into chilled martini glasses. Garnish with a large thin slice of lemon peel.

Jasmine Martini

12 parts Gin
4 parts Triple Sec
4 parts Lime Juice
1 part Campari

Pour ingredients into a shaker with cracked ice and shake well. Strain into chilled martini glasses. Garnish with a lemon twist.

Kermit

3 parts Gin
1 part Pear Liqueur
1 part Blue Curaçao
1 splash of Lemonade

Pour ingredients into a shaker with cracked ice and shake well. Strain into chilled martini glasses. Garnish with a lemon wedge.

Lady Godiva Martini

5 parts Vodka
1 part Godiva White Chocolate Liqueur

Pour ingredients into a shaker with cracked ice and shake well. Strain into chilled martini glasses. Garnish with shaved white chocolate.

Lenin Drop Martini

3 parts Lemon Vodka
3 parts Sour Mix
1 splash Club Soda

Rim glasses with superfine sugar. Pour ingredients into a shaker with cracked ice and shake well. Strain into chilled martini glasses. Garnish with a lemon twist.

Mae West Martini

4 parts Vodka
1 part Melon Liqueur
1 part Amaretto
1 part Cranberry Juice

Pour ingredients into a shaker with cracked ice and shake well. Strain into chilled martini glasses. Garnish with a cherry.

Martini Marilyn

4 parts Vanilla Vodka
2 parts Orange Liqueur
2 parts White Chocolate Liqueur

Pour ingredients into a shaker with cracked ice and shake well. Strain into chilled martini glasses. Garnish with an orange twist and a maraschino cherry.

Martini Navratilova

6 parts Vodka
2 parts Dry Vermouth
1 splash Gatorade (your choice of flavour)
3 dashes Orange Bitters

Pour ingredients into a shaker with cracked ice and shake well. Strain into chilled martini glasses.

Mary Pickford

10 parts White Rum
10 parts Pineapple Juice
1 part Grenadine Syrup

Pour ingredients into a shaker with cracked ice and shake well. Strain into chilled martini glasses.

Mauri Martini

4 parts Pepper Vodka
4 parts Silver Patron
1 part brine from Cocktail Onions
1 squeeze of lemon juice

Pour ingredients into a shaker with cracked ice and shake well. Strain into chilled martini glasses. Garnish with an onion.

Melrose Martini

4 parts Vodka
1 part Triple Sec
1 part Cranberry Juice

Pour ingredients into a shaker with cracked ice and shake well. Strain into chilled martini glasses. Garnish with an orange wedge.

Mick Jagger-meister

1 part Vodka
1 part Jägermeister
1 splash Sour Mix

Pour ingredients into a shaker with cracked ice and shake well. Strain into chilled martini glasses. Garnish with an orange slice.

Moll Flanders Martini

2 parts Gin
1 part Sloe Gin
1 part Dry Vermouth
5 dashes Bitters

Pour ingredients into a shaker with cracked ice and shake well. Strain into chilled martini glasses. Garnish with a lemon twist.

Money Penny Martini

3 parts Vodka
1 part Raspberry Liqueur
1 part Cranberry Juice

Pour ingredients into a shaker with cracked ice and shake well. Strain into chilled martini glasses. Garnish with a cherry.

Money Penny Martini 2

5 parts Vodka
2 parts Raspberry Liqueur
1 part Cranberry Juice

Pour ingredients into a shaker with cracked ice and shake well. Strain into chilled martini glasses. Garnish with a cherry.

Mrs. Robinson Martini

8 parts Vodka
1 part Lemon Liqueur
1 part Orange Juice

Pour ingredients into a shaker with cracked ice and shake well. Strain into chilled martini glasses. Garnish with an orange slice.

Nicky Finn Martini

8 parts Vodka
8 parts Brandy
8 parts Triple Sec
8 parts Lemon Juice
1 part Pernod

Pour ingredients into a shaker with cracked ice and shake well. Strain into chilled martini glasses. Garnish with a cherry and a lime twist.

Northern Exposure Moose Martini

6 parts Vodka
1 part Raspberry Liqueur

Pour ingredients into a shaker with cracked ice and shake well. Strain into chilled martini glasses. Garnish with vermouth soaked juniper berries.

Ozzie's Peach Martini

8 parts Peach Vodka
3 parts Triple Sec
1 part Fresh Lemon Juice

Pour ingredients into a shaker with cracked ice and shake well. Strain into chilled martini glasses.

Peggy Sue's Martini

12 parts Gin
2 parts Sweet Vermouth
1 part Dubonnet Rouge
1 part Pernod

Pour ingredients into a shaker with cracked ice and shake well. Strain into chilled martini glasses. Garnish with a lemon twist.

Pretty Woman Martini

4 parts Vodka
1 part Triple Sec
1 part Amaretto
1 part Dry Vermouth

Pour ingredients into a shaker with cracked ice and shake well. Strain into chilled martini glasses. Garnish with an orange twist.

Prince Edward Martini

6 parts Gin
1 part Drambuie

Pour ingredients into a shaker with cracked ice and shake well. Strain into chilled martini glasses. Garnish with a lemon twist.

Princess Elizabeth

6 parts Sweet Vermouth
1 part Dry Vermouth
1 part Bénédictine

Pour ingredients into a shaker with cracked ice and shake well. Strain into chilled martini glasses. Garnish with a lemon twist.

P.T. Barnum

6 parts Gin
1 part Apricot Brandy
5 dashes Bitters
5 dashes Lemon Juice

Pour ingredients into a shaker with cracked ice and shake well. Strain into chilled martini glasses. Garnish with a lemon twist.

Purple Haze Martini

5 parts Vodka
8 parts Cranberry Juice
2 parts Blue Curaçao
1 part Blackberry Liqueur

Pour ingredients into a shaker with cracked ice and shake well. Strain into chilled martini glasses. Garnish with frozen cranberries.

Purple People Eater

8 parts Limon Bacardi Rum
10 parts Cranberry Juice
1 part Blue Curaçao
1 part Dry Vermouth

Pour ingredients into a shaker with cracked ice and shake well. Strain into chilled martini glasses. Garnish with cranberries.

Q Martini

8 parts Vodka
1 Part Blue Curaçao

Pour ingredients into a shaker with cracked ice and shake well. Strain into chilled martini glasses.

Queen Elizabeth Martini

6 parts Gin
1 part Dry Vermouth
1 part Bénédictine

Pour ingredients into a shaker with cracked ice and shake well. Strain into chilled martini glasses. Garnish with a lemon twist.

Ralph Furley

6 parts Gin
4 parts Orange Juice
1 part Sweet Vermouth
1 part Lime Juice

Pour ingredients into a shaker with cracked ice and shake well. Strain into chilled martini glasses.

Red Beard Martini

5 parts Vodka
4 parts Crème de Cacao
1 part Cranberry Liqueur

Pour ingredients into a shaker with cracked ice and shake well. Strain into chilled martini glasses. Garnish with a lemon twist.

Road Runner Martini

6 parts Pepper Vodka
1 part Dry Vermouth
1 part Gold Tequila

Pour ingredients into a shaker with cracked ice and shake well. Strain into chilled martini glasses. Garnish with a jalapeno stuffed olive.

Rocky's Caesar Martini

4 parts Infused Vodka
5 parts Clamato Juice
1 dash Tabasco Sauce
1 dash Worcestershire Sauce
Fresh Ground Black Pepper

To infuse vodka: Infuse 26oz. of Vodka with red peppers, 2 cloves of fresh garlic, half of a white onion (sliced), 2 stalks of celery (chopped), 2 peeled carrots (shredded) and a chopped jalapeno pepper. Rim chilled martini glasses with celery salt. Pour ingredients except black pepper into a shaker with cracked ice and shake well. Strain into chilled martini glasses. Pepper each glass and garnish with thin slices of celery or spiced green bean and a lime wedge.

Romulan

1 part Lemon Vodka
1 part Raspberry Vodka
1 part Blue Curaçao

Pour ingredients into a shaker with cracked ice and shake well. Strain into chilled martini glasses. Garnish with an orange twist.

Roselyn Martini

8 parts Gin
4 parts Dry Vermouth
1 part Grenadine Syrup

Pour ingredients into a shaker with cracked ice and shake well. Strain into chilled martini glasses.

The Sex and the City Flirtini

3 parts Vodka
1 part Raspberry Liqueur
4 parts Champagne
1 splash Pineapple Juice

Pour ingredients into a shaker with cracked ice and shake well. Strain into chilled martini glasses. Garnish with a pineapple wedge and maraschino cherry.

Tony Soprano Martini

4 parts Gin
1 part Lemoncella

Pour ingredients into a shaker with cracked ice and shake well. Strain into chilled martini glasses. Garnish with a lemon slice.

Wae Lin

8 parts Vodka
1 part Cranberry Juice
1 part Melon Liqueur

Pour ingredients into a shaker with cracked ice and shake well. Strain into chilled martini glasses. Garnish with a lemon twist.

Wembley Martini

6 parts Gin
1 part Dry Vermouth
1 tsp Apricot Brandy
1 tsp Calvados

Pour ingredients into a shaker with cracked ice and shake well. Strain into chilled martini glasses. Garnish with a lemon twist.

Xena Martini

5 parts Honey Vodka
1 part Buffalo Grass Vodka
1 tsp Lillet Blanc

Pour ingredients into a shaker with cracked ice and shake well. Strain into chilled martini glasses. Garnish with a spear of pickled asparagus.

Yellow Submarine

3 parts Vodka
3 parts White Rum
1 part Banana Liqueur

Pour ingredients into a shaker with cracked ice and shake well. Strain into chilled martini glasses. Garnish with banana slices. *Hint: to keep banana slices from browning, toss with fresh lemon juice and keep chilled.*

> "Happiness is a dry martini and a good woman...
> Or a bad woman."
> — George Burns —

Baby Blue Martini

1 part Vodka
1 part Blue Curaçao
1 part Sour Mix

Pour vodka and curaçao into a shaker with cracked ice and shake well. Strain into chilled martini glasses. Mist drinks with sour mix. Garnish with a cherry.

Bagan Blue Martini

5 parts Vodka
2 parts White Rum
1 part Blue Curaçao
1 part Sweet Vermouth

Pour vodka and curaçao into a shaker with cracked ice and shake well. Strain into chilled martini glasses. Garnish with a lemon wedge.

Berry Blue Martini

2 parts Gin
1 part Blue Curaçao
1 part Chambord

Pour ingredients into a shaker with cracked ice and shake well. Strain into chilled martini glasses. Garnish with frozen raspberries and blueberries.

Blue Bayou

4 parts Vodka
3 parts Dry Vermouth
1 part Blue Curaçao
1 splash Cranberry or Lemon Juice (to taste)

Pour ingredients into a shaker with cracked ice and shake well. Strain into chilled martini glasses. Garnish with a lemon twist.

Blue Dolphin Martini

4 parts Vodka
1 part Blue Curaçao
1 part Grapefruit Juice

Pour ingredients into a shaker with cracked ice and shake well. Strain into chilled martini glasses. Garnish with a lemon twist.

Blue Flame

1 part Vodka
1 part Blue Curaçao

Pour ingredients into a shaker with cracked ice and shake well. Strain into chilled martini glasses. Garnish with a lemon twist.

Blue Hawaii Martini

4 parts Vodka
2 parts Dark Rum
2 parts Light Rum
1 part Blue Curaçao
1 part Pineapple Juice

Pour ingredients into a shaker with cracked ice and shake well. Strain into chilled martini glasses. Garnish with a pineapple wedge and a cherry.

Blue Lady Martini

4 parts Gin
2 parts Blue Curaçao
1 part Lemon Juice

Pour ingredients into a shaker with cracked ice and shake well. Strain into chilled martini glasses. Garnish with a lemon twist.

Blue Lagoon

4 parts Vodka
1 part Blue Curaçao
1 part Triple Sec
1 part Lime Cordial
1 part Cranberry Juice
1 splash Melon Liqueur
1 dash Cinnamon Liqueur

Rim martini glasses with an orange zest. Pour ingredients into a shaker with cracked ice and shake well. Strain into chilled martini glasses. Garnish with an orange twist. This is a very smooth drink and it is the colour of a blue lagoon.

Blue Marlin Martini

3 parts Vodka
1 part Blue Curaçao
1 part Light Rum
4 parts Lemon-Lime Juice

Pour ingredients into a shaker with cracked ice and shake well. Strain into chilled martini glasses. Garnish with a lemon twist.

Blue Monday

2 parts Vodka
1 part Triple Sec
1 dash Blue Food Colouring

Pour ingredients into a shaker with cracked ice and shake well. Strain into chilled martini glasses. Garnish with an orange twist.

Blue Moon Martini

6 parts Gin
1 part Blue Curaçao

Pour ingredients into a shaker with cracked ice and shake well. Strain into chilled martini glasses. Garnish with a floating lemon wheel.

Blue on Blue Martini

6 parts Vodka
1 part Blue Curaçao

Pour ingredients into a shaker with cracked ice and shake well. Strain into chilled martini glasses. Garnish with an olive.

Blue Velvet Martini

10 parts Vodka
1 part Blue Curaçao
2 parts Lime Juice

Pour ingredients into a shaker with cracked ice and shake well. Strain into chilled martini glasses. Garnish with a lemon wedge.

Blueberry Martini

1 part Vodka or Gin
1 part Blueberry Schnapps

Pour ingredients into a shaker with cracked ice and shake well. Strain into chilled martini glasses. Garnish with a lemon twist and frozen whole blueberries.

Blues Martini

1 part Vodka
1 part Gin
1 dash Blue Curaçao

Pour ingredients into a shaker with cracked ice and shake well. Strain into chilled martini glasses.

Bombay Blue

2 parts Gin
1 part Dry Vermouth
1 splash Blue Curaçao

Pour ingredients into a shaker with cracked ice and shake well. Strain into chilled martini glasses. Garnish with a lemon twist.

Little Boy Blue

8 parts Gin
1 part Blue Curaçao

Pour gin into a shaker with cracked ice and place in freezer for 15 minutes. Remove from freezer, add blue curaçao and shake well. Strain into chilled martini glasses. Garnish with a lemon peel. Serve immediately.

Lizzy's Blue Eyes

2 parts Vodka
1 part Blue Curaçao
1 part Orange Liqueur

Pour ingredients into a shaker with cracked ice and shake well. Strain into chilled martini glasses. Garnish with an orange slice.

Tidy Bowl

1 part Coconut Rum
1 part Blue Curaçao
1 part Pineapple Juice

Pour Rum and Blue Curaçao into a shaker with cracked ice and shake well. Strain into chilled martini glasses. Slowly pour Pineapple Juice down the side of glass to layer. Float a pineapple ring on top.

Vanilla Skies

3 parts Vanilla Vodka
1 part Blue Curaçao

Pour ingredients into a shaker with cracked ice and shake well. Strain into chilled martini glasses. Garnish with an orange wedge.

THE INTERNATIONALS

"I'm not talking a cup of cheap gin splashed over
an ice cube. I'm talking satin, fire and ice;
Fred Astaire in a glass; surgical cleanliness; insight
and comfort; redemption and absolution.
I'm talking a Martini."

— unknown —

Bermuda Triangle

4 parts Vodka
2 parts Peach Schnapps
1 part Banana Liqueur
1 part Almond Liqueur
2 parts Orange Juice
2 parts Pineapple Juice
2 parts Cranberry Juice

Pour ingredients into a shaker with cracked ice and shake well. Strain into chilled martini glasses. Garnish with an orange wedge.

Biscayne Bay Martini

3 parts Vodka
3 parts Bacardi Limon Rum
1 part Blue Curaçao
6 parts Sour Mix

Pour ingredients into a chilled shaker with cracked ice and shake well. Strain into chilled martini glasses. Garnish with a lemon twist.

California Martini

6 parts Vodka
1 part Red Wine
1 part Dark Rum
5 dashes Bitters

Pour all ingredients into a shaker with cracked ice and shake well. Strain into chilled martini glasses. Garnish with an orange twist.

Cape Cod Bellini

4 parts Spumante Champagne
1 part Vodka
1 part Chambord

Pour Champagne into chilled martini glass. Pour remaining ingredients into a shaker with cracked ice and shake well. Strain into Champagne. Garnish with a fresh raspberry.

Caribbean Queen

2 parts Vodka
1 part Coconut Rum
1 part Peach Schnapps
1 part Banana Liqueur

Pour all ingredients into a shaker with cracked ice and shake well. Strain into chilled martini glasses. Garnish with a slice of banana.

Caribbean Surfer

2 parts White Rum
1 part Coconut Rum
1 part Banana Liqueur
2 parts Pineapple Juice

Pour all ingredients into a shaker with cracked ice and shake well. Strain into chilled martini glasses. Garnish with a pineapple wedge.

Champs Elysees Martini

4 parts Vodka
4 parts Cognac
1 part Green Chartreuse
4 parts Lemon Juice
2 drops Bitters

Pour all ingredients into a shaker with cracked ice and shake well. Strain into chilled martini glasses. Garnish with a lemon twist.

Crazy Fin

6 parts Vodka
3 parts Fino Sherry
3 parts Triple Sec
1 part Lemon Juice

Pour all ingredients into a shaker with cracked ice and shake well. Strain into chilled martini glasses. Garnish with a lemon twist.

Cuban Martini

6 parts Light Rum
1 part Dry Vermouth

Rim chilled martini glasses with sugar. Pour all ingredients into a shaker with cracked ice and shake well. Strain into prepared martini glasses. Garnish with a lime twist.

Danish Martini

6 parts of Aquivit
1 part Dry Vermouth

Pour all ingredients into a shaker with cracked ice and shake well. Strain into chilled martini glasses. Garnish with an olive.

Europa Martini

4 parts Vodka
1 part Pernod
1 part Cranberry Juice

Pour all ingredients into a shaker with cracked ice and shake well. Strain into chilled martini glasses. Garnish with a lemon twist.

European Thunder Martini

4 parts Vodka
1 part Whiskey Liqueur
1 part Raspberry Schnapps
1 part Cranberry Juice
1 part Lime Juice

Pour all ingredients into a shaker with cracked ice and shake well. Strain into chilled martini glasses. Garnish with a lime wedge.

Florida Twist Martini

1 part Orange Vodka
1 part Citron Vodka

Pour ingredients into a shaker with cracked ice and shake well. Strain into chilled martini glasses. Garnish with an orange twist.

Great Canadian Martini

1 part Vodka
1 part Maple Liqueur

Pour all ingredients into a shaker with cracked ice and shake well. Strain into chilled martini glasses. Garnish with a cherry.

Hawaiiantini

6 parts Vodka
2 parts Pineapple Juice
1 part Coconut Rum

Rim chilled martini glasses with shaved coconut. Pour ingredients into a shaker with cracked ice and shake well. Strain into chilled martini glasses. Garnish with a pineapple wedge.

Irish Martini

3 parts Irish Whiskey
2 parts Bailey's

Rim chilled martini glasses with cinnamon and sugar. Pour all ingredients into a shaker with cracked ice and shake well. Strain into prepared martini glasses.

Irish Martini 2

6 parts Buffalo Grass Vodka
1 part Dry Vermouth
1 part Irish Whiskey

Pour all ingredients into a shaker with cracked ice and shake well. Strain into chilled martini glasses. Garnish with a lemon twist.

Italian Ice Martini

8 parts Citrus Vodka
1 part Sour Mix

Pour all ingredients into a shaker with cracked ice and shake well. Strain into chilled martini glasses. Garnish with an ice cube and a lemon twist.

Jamaica Me Crazitini

1 part Vodka
1 part Amber Rum
1 part Tia Maria
3 parts Pineapple Juice

Pour all ingredients into a shaker with cracked ice and shake well. Strain into chilled martini glasses. Garnish with cherry peppers.

Jamaican Martini

6 parts Gin
1 part Red Wine
1 part Dark Rum
5 dashes Bitters

Pour all ingredients into a shaker with cracked ice and shake well. Strain into chilled martini glasses. Garnish with cherry peppers.

Kyoto Martini

6 parts Gin
2 parts Melon Liqueur
1 part Dry Vermouth
1/4 tsp Lemon Juice

Pour ingredients into a shaker with cracked ice and shake well. Strain into chilled martini glasses. Garnish with melon balls.

Latino Lactation

10 parts Vodka
2 parts Hazelnut Liqueur
2 parts Crème de Cacao
1 part Bailey's

Pour ingredients into a shaker with cracked ice and shake well.
Strain into chilled martini glasses. Garnish with roasted pine nuts.

London Martini

6 parts Gin
1 part Maraschino Liqueur
5 dashes Bitters
1/2 tsp Bar Sugar

Pour ingredients into a shaker with cracked ice and shake well.
Strain into chilled martini glasses. Garnish with a lemon twist.

Mayan Martini

2 parts Vodka
3 parts Espresso
1 part White Crème de Cacao

Pour ingredients into a shaker with cracked ice and shake well.
Strain into chilled martini glasses. Garnish with a cherry.

Mexican Greyhound

3 parts Vodka
1 part Grapefruit Juice

Pour ingredients into a shaker with cracked ice and shake well.
Strain into chilled martini glasses. Garnish with a grapefruit twist.

Mexican Martini

3 parts Vodka
1 part Lime Juice
3 parts Corona

Rim chilled martini glasses with salt. Pour all ingredients except
Corona into a shaker with cracked ice and shake well. Strain into prepared martini glasses. Top with Corona and garnish with a lime
wedge.

Mexican Water Martini

1 part Tequila
1 part Lime Juice

Rim chilled martini glasses with salt. Pour ingredients into a shaker with cracked ice and shake well. Strain into prepared martini glasses. Garnish with a lime wedge.

Milano Martini

8 parts Gin
2 parts Dry Vermouth
2 parts White Wine
1 part Campari

Pour all ingredients into a shaker with cracked ice and shake well. Strain into chilled martini glasses. Garnish with a lime twist.

Milano Martini 2

3 parts Gin
2 parts Galliano
1 part Lemon Juice

Pour all ingredients into a shaker with cracked ice and shake well. Strain into chilled martini glasses. Garnish with a lemon twist.

Montanatini

2 parts Vodka
1 part Cranberry Juice
1 splash Grape Concentrate
1 splash Peach Concentrate

Pour ingredients into a shaker with cracked ice and shake well. Strain into chilled martini glasses. Garnish with pomegranate seeds.

New Orleans Martini

6 parts Vanilla Vodka
1 part Dry Vermouth
1 part Pernod
1 dash Bitters

Pour ingredients into a shaker with cracked ice and shake well. Strain into chilled martini glasses. Garnish with a mint sprig.

Osaka Dry Martini

6 parts Vodka
1 part Saké

Pour all ingredients into a shaker with cracked ice and shake well. Strain into chilled martini glasses. Garnish with a pickled plum.

Palm Beach Martini

6 parts Gin
1 part Sweet Vermouth
4 parts Grapefruit Juice

Pour ingredients into a shaker with cracked ice and shake well.
Strain into chilled martini glasses. Garnish with a grapefruit twist.

Parisan Martini

6 parts Gin
2 parts Dry Vermouth
1 part Crème de Cassis

Pour all ingredients into a shaker with cracked ice and shake well.
Strain into chilled martini glasses. Garnish with a lemon twist.

Park Avenue Martini

6 parts Gin
1 part Sweet Vermouth
1 part Pineapple Juice

Pour ingredients into a shaker with cracked ice and shake well.
Strain into chilled martini glasses. Garnish with a pineapple wedge.

Russian Martini

4 parts Gin
4 parts Godiva White Chocolate Liqueur

Pour ingredients into a shaker with cracked ice and shake well.
Strain into chilled martini glasses.

Russian River Martini

5 parts Vodka
3 parts Whiskey Liqueur
5 parts Cranberry Juice
3 parts Sour Mix
1 part Lime Cordial

Pour ingredients into a shaker with cracked ice and shake well.
Strain into chilled martini glasses. Garnish with a lemon wedge.

Russian Rose

6 parts Strawberry Vodka
1 part Dry Vermouth
1 part Grenadine
1 dash Bitters

Pour ingredients into a shaker with cracked ice and shake well.
Strain into chilled martini glasses. Garnish with a lemon twist.

St. Petersburg Martini

1 part Vodka
5 dashes Bitters

Pour ingredients into a shaker with cracked ice and shake well. Strain into chilled martini glasses. Garnish with an orange peel.

Soviet Martini

8 parts Vodka
4 parts Manzanilla Sherry
1 part Dry Vermouth

Pour ingredients into a shaker with cracked ice and shake well. Strain into chilled martini glasses. Garnish with a lemon twist.

Soviet Martini 2

6 parts Ashberry or Currant Vodka
1 part Dry Vermouth
1 part Fino Sherry

Pour ingredients into a shaker with cracked ice and shake well. Strain into chilled martini glasses. Garnish with a lemon twist.

Stockholm

3 parts Lemon Vodka
2 parts Lemon Juice
1 part Sugar Syrup
1 splash Champagne

Rim chilled martini glasses with sugar. Pour all ingredients except Champagne into a shaker with cracked ice and shake well. Strain into prepared martini glasses. Top with Champagne.

Valencia Martini

3 parts Gin
1 part Amontillado Sherry

Pour ingredients into a shaker with cracked ice and shake well. Strain into chilled martini glasses. Garnish with an olive.

Waikiki Martini

6 parts Pineapple Vodka
1 part Dry Vermouth
1 part Lillet Blanc

Pour ingredients into a shaker with cracked ice and shake well. Strain into chilled martini glasses. Garnish with a pineapple wedge.

Waldorf Martini

5 parts Vodka
1 part Triple Sec
1 part Lime Juice

Pour ingredients into a shaker with cracked ice and shake well. Strain into chilled martini glasses. Garnish with lemon and lime twists.

West Coast Caesar

1 part Vodka

Rim chilled martini glasses with celery salt. Pour chilled vodka into glasses. Garnish with a skewer of capers, fresh garlic, lox and a wedge of lemon.

*"I have taken more good from alcohol
than alcohol has taken from me."*

— Winston Churchill —

THE COSMOPOLITANS

"...let me fix you a Martini that's pure magic.
It may not make life's problems disappear,
but it'll certainly reduce their size."

— Some Came Running 1959 —
(starring Frank Sinatra & Dean Martin)

Barney's Cosmopolitan

4 parts Vodka
1 part Blue Curaçao
3 parts Cranberry Juice
2 parts Lime Juice

Pour ingredients into a shaker with cracked ice and shake well. Strain into chilled martini glasses. Garnish with a lemon twist.

Citrus Cosmopolitan

2 parts Lemon Vodka
1 part Triple Sec
1 splash Lime Juice
1 splash Cranberry Juice

Pour ingredients into a shaker with cracked ice and shake well. Strain into chilled martini glasses. Garnish with a lime twist.

Cosmopolitan Martini

8 parts Vodka
2 parts Cranberry Juice
1 part Lime Cordial
1 part Triple Sec

Pour ingredients into a shaker with cracked ice and shake well. Strain into chilled martini glasses. Garnish with a lemon twist.

Cosmopolitan Martini 2

4 parts Citron Vodka
3 parts Triple Sec
1 part Cranberry Juice
1 part Lemon Juice

Pour ingredients into a shaker with cracked ice and shake well. Strain into chilled martini glasses. Garnish with a lemon wedge.

Cosmopolitan Martini 3

2 parts Vodka
1 part Triple Sec
1 part Lime Cordial
1 part Cranberry Juice

Rim glasses with fresh lime wedge. Pour ingredients into a shaker with cracked ice and shake well. Strain into chilled martini glasses. Garnish with a lime wedge.

Cosmopolitan Martini 4

8 parts Vodka
4 parts Triple Sec
1 part Lime Juice

Pour ingredients into a shaker with cracked ice and shake well. Strain into chilled martini glasses. Garnish with a lemon twist.

Cosmopolitan Martini 5

8 parts Vodka
8 parts Cranberry Juice
4 parts Lime Juice
3 parts Grand Marnier

Pour ingredients into a shaker with cracked ice and shake well. Strain into chilled martini glasses. Garnish with a lime twist.

Cupid's Cosmicpolitan

8 parts Cranberry Juice
3 parts Vodka
2 parts Grand Marnier
1 part Lemon Juice

Pour ingredients into a shaker with cracked ice and shake well. Strain into chilled martini glasses. Garnish with a maraschino cherry.

Down Town Cosmopolitan

6 parts Citron Vodka
2 parts Triple Sec
2 parts Lime Juice
1 part Cranberry Juice

Pour ingredients into a shaker with cracked ice and shake well. Strain into chilled martini glasses. Garnish with a lime twist.

Educated Cosmopolitan

4 parts Vodka
1 part Triple Sec
1 part Lime Juice
2 parts Cranberry Juice
1 part Raspberry Liqueur

Pour ingredients into a shaker with cracked ice and shake well. Strain into chilled martini glasses. Garnish with purple grapes.

Ginger Cosmopolitan

4 parts Ginger Infused Vodka
2 parts Triple Sec
2 parts Cranberry Juice
1 part Fresh Lime Juice

To infuse vodka: In an airtight container place 4 oz of fresh chopped ginger root, pour in 16 oz of Vodka. Seal container and shake well 3 - 5 times. Let stand in a cool dark place 24 hours. Shake well again and let stand an additional 24 hours. Strain into another container and chill. If a stronger flavour is desired let stand for longer period of time shaking once a day. Pour ingredients into a shaker with cracked ice and shake well. Strain into chilled martini glasses. Garnish with an orange wedge.

Kamikazi Cosmopolitan

4 parts Vodka
2 parts Triple Sec
2 parts Lime Juice
2 parts Cranberry Juice
3 parts Peach Schnapps

Pour ingredients into a shaker with cracked ice and shake well. Strain into chilled martini glasses. Garnish with a peach slice.

Limon Cosmopolitan

8 parts Limon Rum
4 parts Triple Sec
1 part Lime Juice

Pour ingredients into a shaker with cracked ice and shake well. Strain into chilled martini glasses. Garnish with a lime twist.

Monday Cosmopolitan

4 parts Vodka
2 parts Extra Dry Vermouth
2 parts Cranberry Juice
1 part Orange Liqueur

Pour ingredients into a shaker with cracked ice and shake well. Strain into chilled martini glasses. Garnish with an orange slice.

Plum Cosmopolitan

2 parts Vodka
1 part Triple Sec
2 parts Plum Juice
2 parts Cran-Raspberry Juice
1 dash Angostura Bitters

Pour ingredients into a shaker with cracked ice and shake well. Strain into chilled martini glasses. Garnish with raspberries and a lemon twist.

Ultimate Cosmopolitan

3 parts Citron Vodka
2 parts Triple Sec
2 parts Cranberry Juice
1 splash Lime Juice

Pour ingredients into a shaker with cracked ice and shake well. Strain into chilled martini glasses. Garnish with a lime twist.

THE FRUIT MARTINIS

*"The problem with the world is
that everyone is a few drinks behind"*

— Humphrey Bogart —

Absolut Crantini

3 parts Currant Vodka
1 part Crème de Cassis
4 parts Cranberry Juice
1 splash Lemon Juice

Pour ingredients into a shaker with cracked ice and shake well. Strain into chilled martini glasses. Garnish with fresh cranberries.

Absolutely Watermelon

2 parts Watermelon Pucker
1 part Currant Vodka

Pour ingredients into a shaker with cracked ice and shake well. Strain into chilled martini glasses. Garnish with thinly sliced watermelon wedges or frozen watermelon balls.

Alize Tropic Martini

5 parts Alize Red Passion Liqueur
1 part Coconut Rum

Pour ingredients into a shaker with cracked ice and shake well. Strain into chilled martini glasses. Garnish with a maraschino cherry.

Aloha

6 parts Vodka
3 parts Pineapple Juice
3 parts Apricot Brandy

Pour ingredients into a shaker with cracked ice and shake well. Strain into chilled martini glasses. Garnish with a pineapple wedge.

Apple-licious Martini

3 parts Citron Vodka
3 parts Sour Apple Liqueur
1 splash of Sprite

Rim chilled martini glasses with sugar. Pour Vodka and Sour Apple Liqueur into a shaker with cracked ice and shake well. Strain into prepared martini glasses. Top with a splash of Sprite.

Apple Midoritini

2 parts Vodka
1 part Sour Apple Liqueur
1 splash Midori Melon Liqueur

Pour ingredients into a shaker with cracked ice and shake well. Strain into chilled martini glasses. Float a thin round slice of apple on top of martini and place a cherry in the centre of the apple slice.

Apple Sauce Martini

4 parts Vodka
1 part Apple Brandy

Pour ingredients into a shaker with cracked ice and shake well. Strain into chilled martini glasses. Garnish with an apple slice.

Applebomb

2 parts Sour Apple Schnapps
1 part Vodka
1 splash Sour Mix

Rim chilled martini glasses with white sugar (rub rim with lime or lemon wedge and spin in sugar) set aside. Pour ingredients into a shaker with cracked ice and shake well. Strain into chilled martini glasses. Garnish with thinly sliced Granny Smith Apple rounds.

Appletini

2 parts Vodka
1 part Triple Sec
1 part Sour Apple Schnapps

Pour ingredients into a shaker with cracked ice and shake well. Strain into chilled martini glasses. Garnish with apple slices or wedges.

Apricot Martini

1 part Vodka
1 part Godiva White Chocolate Liqueur
1 part Apricot Brandy

Pour ingredients into a shaker with cracked ice and shake well. Strain into chilled martini glasses. Garnish with a cherry.

Apricot Martini 2

4 parts Brandy
1 part Apricot Brandy
1 part Lemon Juice
1 dash Angostura Bitters

Pour ingredients into a shaker with cracked ice and shake well. Strain into chilled martini glasses. Garnish with an apricot wedge.

Atomic Orange Martini

2 parts Vodka
3 parts Melon Liqueur
4 parts Orange Juice

Pour ingredients into a shaker with cracked ice and shake well. Strain into chilled martini glasses. Garnish with an orange slice.

Baby Baby

2 parts Vodka
1 part Cointreau
2 parts Orange Juice

Pour ingredients into a shaker with cracked ice and shake well. Strain into chilled martini glasses. Garnish with a slice of lime.

Banana Bomb

1 part Vodka
1 part Crème de Bananes
1 splash of Cream
1 splash of Kahlua

Pour ingredients into a shaker with cracked ice and shake well. Strain into chilled martini glasses.

Berritini

6 parts Currant Vodka
1 part Raspberry Eau-de-vie

Pour ingredients into a shaker with cracked ice and shake well. Strain into chilled martini glasses. Garnish with frozen berries.

Berritini 2

6 parts Citron Vodka
3 parts Chambord
1 splash Sweet & Sour Mix

Rim chilled martini glasses with icing sugar. Pour ingredients into a shaker with cracked ice and shake well. Strain into prepared martini glasses. Garnish with a lemon twist.

Berry Berry

2 parts Raspberry Vodka
1 part Raspberry Liqueur
1 splash Cranberry Juice

Pour ingredients into a shaker with cracked ice and shake well. Strain into chilled martini glasses. Garnish with frozen raspberries.

Berry Exciting

2 parts Vodka
1 part Strawberry Schnapps
1 splash Triple Sec
1 dash Fresh Lemon Juice

Pour ingredients into a shaker with cracked ice and shake well. Strain into chilled martini glasses. Garnish with a lemon twist and a fresh strawberry.

Berry Good Martini

1 part Vodka
1 part Raspberry Liqueur
1 part Pineapple Juice

Pour ingredients into a shaker with cracked ice and shake well. Strain into chilled martini glasses. Garnish with lemon and lime slices.

Berry White

4 parts Raspberry Vodka
1 part Triple Sec
1 splash Freshly Squeezed Lime Juice (to taste)

Pour ingredients into a shaker with cracked ice and shake well. Strain into chilled martini glasses. Garnish with fresh blackberries.

Black Martini

10 parts Raspberry Vodka
1 part Chambord

Pour ingredients into a shaker with cracked ice and shake well. Strain into chilled martini glasses. Garnish with frozen raspberries.

Blueberritini

1 part Gin
1 part Berry Vodka
1 part Blueberry Schnapps

Pour ingredients into a shaker with cracked ice and shake well. Strain into chilled martini glasses. Garnish with a lemon twist and frozen whole blueberries.

Cherry Martini

2 parts Vodka
1 part Cherry Brandy

Pour ingredients into a shaker with cracked ice and shake well. Strain into chilled martini glasses. Garnish with a maraschino cherry or a fresh Bing cherry (pitted of course).

Citron Dragon

3 parts Citron Vodka
2 parts Midori Melon Liqueur
1 part Lemon Juice

Rim chilled martini glasses with sugar. Pour ingredients into a shaker with cracked ice and shake well. Strain into prepared glasses. Garnish with a lemon twist.

Citrontini

9 parts Citron Vodka
1 part Lemon Juice
2 parts Sour Mix

Pour ingredients into a shaker with cracked ice and shake well. Strain into chilled martini glasses. Garnish with a lemon twist.

Citrus Martini

8 parts Lemon Vodka
1 part Triple Sec
1 part Lime Juice

Pour ingredients into a shaker with cracked ice and shake well. Strain into chilled martini glasses. Garnish with an orange wheel or a lime twist.

Citrus Groves Martini

4 parts Orange Vodka
2 parts Orange Liqueur
2 parts Pineapple Juice
2 parts Cranberry Juice
1 part Sour Mix

Pour ingredients into a shaker with cracked ice and shake well. Strain into chilled martini glasses. Garnish with an orange twist.

Cloudbuster

2 parts Vodka
1 part Melon Liqueur

Pour ingredients into a shaker with cracked ice and shake well. Strain into chilled martini glasses. Garnish with honeydew melon balls and a lemon twist.

Cranberry Martini

6 parts Vodka
8 parts Cranberry Juice
1 part Lime Cordial

Pour ingredients into a shaker with cracked ice and shake well. Strain into chilled martini glasses. Garnish with a lime wedge.

Crantini

2 parts Cranberry Vodka
1 part Cranberry Juice

Pour ingredients into a shaker with cracked ice and shake well. Strain into chilled martini glasses. Garnish with fresh cranberries.

Crantini 2

6 parts Gin
1 part Cranberry Juice

Pour ingredients into a shaker with cracked ice and shake well. Strain into chilled martini glasses. Garnish with a lemon twist.

Currantly Hazey Martini

2 parts Currant Vodka
1 part Raspberry Liqueur
1 part Champagne

Rub inside of a chilled martini glass with lemon. Pour Vodka and Raspberry Liqueur into a shaker with cracked ice and shake well. Strain into prepared martini glasses. Top with Champagne. Garnish with a lemon twist.

Disco Daze

8 parts Raspberry Vodka
3 parts Blue Curaçao
8 parts Lemonade
1 splash Orange Juice

Pour ingredients into a shaker with cracked ice and shake well. Strain into chilled martini glasses. Garnish with a cherry.

Dragon Cider Martini

3 parts Vodka
1 part Cinnamon Schnapps
2 parts Apple Cider

Pour ingredients into a shaker with cracked ice and shake well. Strain into chilled martini glasses. Garnish with an apple slice.

Eden Martini

1 part Vodka
1 part Apple Schnapps

Pour ingredients into a shaker with cracked ice and shake well. Strain into chilled martini glasses. Garnish with an apple wedge.

El Nino

2 parts Vodka
2 parts Peach Schnapps
1 part Blue Curaçao
4 parts Pineapple Juice
4 parts Orange Juice
1 splash of Soda Water

Pour ingredients except soda water into a shaker with cracked ice and shake well. Strain into chilled martini glasses add a splash of soda water to each glass and garnish with an orange slice.

Evan Martini

6 parts Vodka
3 parts Triple Sec
3 parts Lemon Juice
1 part Cranberry Juice

Pour ingredients into a shaker with cracked ice and shake well. Strain into chilled martini glasses. Garnish with a lemon twist and an orange wedge.

Fanmango

2 parts Vodka
1 part Apricot Brandy
1 part Mango Juice
1 part Tangerine Juice
1 part Cranberry Juice

Pour ingredients into a shaker with cracked ice and shake well. Strain into chilled martini glasses. Garnish with a sugared star fruit.

Forever Tango Martini

1 part Lime Gin
1 part Citron Vodka

Pour ingredients into a shaker with cracked ice and shake well. Strain into chilled martini glasses. Garnish with a lemon twist.

Fruit Salad Martini

1 part Vodka
2 parts Sour Apple Schnapps
2 parts Banana Liqueur

Pour ingredients into a shaker with cracked ice and shake well. Strain into chilled martini glasses. Garnish with a slice of banana, a slice of apple and a fresh strawberry.

Fuzzy Martini

8 parts Vanilla Vodka
2 parts Coffee Vodka
1 part Peach Schnapps

Pour ingredients into a shaker with cracked ice and shake well. Strain into chilled martini glasses. Garnish with a peach slice.

Girasole

3 parts Orange Vodka
3 parts Orange Juice
1 part Orange Liqueur
1 part Cynar

Pour ingredients into a shaker with cracked ice and shake well. Strain into chilled martini glasses. Garnish with an orange twist.

Glamorous Martini

6 parts Vodka
6 parts Orange Juice
6 parts Grapefruit Juice
1 part Triple Sec

Pour ingredients into a shaker with cracked ice and shake well. Strain into chilled martini glasses. Garnish with an orange slice.

Golden Apple Martini

1 part Galliano Liqueur
1 part Vodka
1 part Sour Apple Schnapps

Pour Galliano into a chilled martini glass. Pour remaining ingredients into a shaker with cracked ice and shake well. Strain into prepared martini glasses. Garnish with an a cinnamon stick.

Grand Crantini

3 parts Cranberry Vodka
1 part Grand Marnier

Pour ingredients into a shaker with cracked ice and shake well. Strain into chilled martini glasses. Garnish with an orange twist.

Green Appletini

2 parts Vodka
1 part Cognac
1 part Lime Cordial
1 dash Lillet

Pour ingredients into a shaker with cracked ice and shake well. Strain into chilled martini glasses. Garnish with green apple slices.

Green Eyes

1 part Vodka
1 part Blue Curaçao
2 parts Orange Juice

Pour ingredients into a shaker with cracked ice and shake well.
Strain into chilled martini glasses. Garnish with a cherry.

Guru Martini

2 parts Vodka
4 parts Gin
2 parts Raspberry Liqueur
1 part Triple Sec
6 parts Cranberry Juice

Pour ingredients into a shaker with cracked ice and shake well.
Strain into chilled martini glasses. Garnish with an orange wedge.

Gypsy Dancer Martini

8 parts Vodka
1 part Melon Liqueur
1 part Lime Cordial

Pour ingredients into a shaker with cracked ice and shake well.
Strain into chilled martini glasses. Garnish with a lime twist.

Honeydew Martini

6 parts Vodka
1 part Midori Melon Liqueur
1 part Triple Sec

Pour ingredients into a shaker with cracked ice and shake well.
Strain into chilled martini glasses. Garnish with a lemon twist and
honeydew melon balls.

Hooch

8 parts Vodka
5 parts Sour Mix
4 parts Cranberry Juice
2 parts Peach Schnapps

Lightly rim chilled martini glasses with sugar. Pour ingredients into a
shaker with cracked ice and shake well. Strain into prepared martini glasses. Garnish with a lemon twist.

Hot Apple Martini

2 parts Vodka
1 part Sour Apple Schnapps
1 splash Cinnamon Liqueur
1 dash Sweet Vermouth

Pour ingredients into a shaker with cracked ice and shake well. Strain into chilled martini glasses. Garnish with a long cinnamon stick and an apple slice.

Hot Date

1 part Vodka
1 part Raspberry Juice
1 splash Sweet Vermouth

Rinse glasses with sweet vermouth. Pour vodka and raspberry juice into a shaker with cracked ice and shake well. Strain into chilled martini glasses. Garnish with a lemon twist.

Hula's Mai Tai Martini

4 parts Vodka
1 part Dry Vermouth
1 part Orange Liqueur
1 part Pineapple Juice
1 part Orgeat Syrup

Pour ingredients into a shaker with cracked ice and shake well. Strain into chilled martini glasses. Garnish with a pineapple slice and a cherry.

In the Sack

6 parts Cream Sherry
6 parts Orange Juice
4 parts Apricot Nectar
1 part Lemon Juice

Pour ingredients into a shaker with cracked ice and shake well. Strain into chilled martini glasses. Garnish with an orange slice.

J&J Martini

6 parts Vodka
1 part Triple Sec
2 parts Orange Juice
1/4 tsp Bar Sugar

Pour ingredients into a shaker with cracked ice and shake well. Strain into chilled martini glasses. Garnish with an orange wedge.

J'kazi Martini

6 parts Vodka
6 parts Cranberry Juice
1 part Cointreau
1 part Lime Juice

Pour ingredients into a shaker with cracked ice and shake well. Strain into chilled martini glasses. Garnish with a lime wedge.

Jolly Apple Martini

1 part Lemon Vodka
3 parts Sour Apple Schnapps
1 part Sour Mix

Pour ingredients into a shaker with cracked ice and shake well. Strain into chilled martini glasses. Garnish with a Granny Smith apple wedge and a lemon twist.

Kurrant Affair Martini

4 parts Currant Vodka
1 part Chambord
1 part Cranberry Juice

Pour ingredients into a shaker with cracked ice and shake well. Strain into chilled martini glasses. Garnish with a lemon twist.

Kurrantini

2 parts Currant Vodka
1 part Dry Vermouth
1 part Black Currant Liqueur

Coat chilled martini glasses with Black Currant Liqueur. Pour ingredients into a shaker with cracked ice and shake well. Strain into chilled martini glasses. Garnish with black currants.

Lemon Aid

1 part Vodka
1 part Lemon Liqueur

Pour ingredients into a shaker with cracked ice and shake well. Strain into chilled martini glasses. Garnish with a lemon slice.

Lemon Blue Martini

4 parts Vodka
4 parts Gin
3 parts Blue Curaçao

Pour ingredients into a shaker with cracked ice and shake well. Strain into chilled martini glasses. Garnish with a lemon wedge.

Lime Light Martini

6 parts Vodka
1 part Triple Sec
1 part Grapefruit Juice

Pour ingredients into a shaker with cracked ice and shake well. Strain into chilled martini glasses. Garnish with a grapefruit twist.

Lime Lighter

3 parts Vodka
1 part Melon Liqueur
1 part Grapefruit Juice
1 splash Lime Juice
1 dash Sour Mix

Pour ingredients into a shaker with cracked ice and shake well. Strain into chilled martini glasses. Garnish with a lime wedge.

Lime Lighter 2

1 part Vodka
2 parts Melon Liqueur
1 splash Grapefruit Juice

Pour ingredients into a shaker with cracked ice and shake well. Strain into chilled martini glasses. Garnish with a lime wedge. *Note: This martini turns out to be a glowing neon green.*

Limon Crantini

8 parts Bacardi Limon Rum
4 parts Triple Sec
1 part Cranberry Juice

Pour ingredients into a shaker with cracked ice and shake well. Strain into chilled martini glasses. Garnish with a lemon twist.

Lychee Martini

2 parts Vodka
1 part Lychee Liqueur
2 drops Crème de Cassis

Pour Vodka and Lychee Liqueur into a shaker with cracked ice and shake well. Strain into chilled martini glasses. Drop two drops of Crème de Cassis into each glass. Garnish with a slice of lychee fruit.

Madras Martini

5 parts Orange Vodka
1 part Cranberry Juice

Pour ingredients into a shaker with cracked ice and shake well. Strain into chilled martini glasses. Garnish with an orange twist.

Maiden's Prayer

1 part Gin
1 part White Rum
1 part Orange Juice
1 part Lemon Juice

Pour ingredients into a shaker with cracked ice and shake well. Strain into chilled martini glasses. Garnish with an orange twist.

Mandarin Martini

8 parts Mandarin Orange Vodka
4 parts Gin
3 parts Triple Sec
4 parts Sour Mix
1 Splash Pineapple Juice

Pour ingredients into a shaker with cracked ice and shake well. Strain into chilled martini glasses. Garnish with frozen mandarin wedges and orange and lemon twists.

Mango Madness

2 parts Vodka
1 part Melon Liqueur
1 splash Mango Juice

Pour Vodka and Melon Liqueur into a shaker with cracked ice and shake well. Strain into chilled martini glasses. Fill glasses to just below the rim with mango juice. Garnish with a mango wedge.

Marstini

4 parts Vodka
2 parts Peach Schnapps
2 parts Apple Liqueur
4 parts Grapefruit Juice
1 dash Grenadine

Pour all ingredients except grenadine into a shaker with cracked ice and shake well. Strain into chilled martini glasses. Dash with grenadine. Garnish with a pomegranate wedge.

Melancholy Martini

2 parts Vodka
1 part Lemon Liqueur

Pour ingredients into a shaker with cracked ice and shake well. Strain into chilled martini glasses. Garnish with a fresh strawberry.

Mellasara

2 parts Raspberry Vodka
4 parts Melon Liqueur
1 splash of Lemon Lime Soda

Pour all ingredients except Soda into a shaker with cracked ice and shake well. Strain into chilled martini glasses. Top with soda. Garnish with a lime twist.

Melon Ball

3 parts Gin
2 parts Melon Liqueur
1 part Vodka

Pour ingredients into a shaker with cracked ice and shake well. Strain into chilled martini glasses. Garnish with frozen honeydew melon balls.

Melon Martini

6 parts Vodka
2 parts Midori Melon Liqueur
1 part Lime Juice

Pour ingredients into a shaker with cracked ice and shake well. Strain into chilled martini glasses. Garnish with a melon slice.

Melon Pineapple Martini

3 parts Vodka
3 parts Pineapple Juice
2 parts Melon Liqueur

Pour ingredients into a shaker with cracked ice and shake well. Strain into chilled martini glasses. Garnish with fresh melon balls and chunks of pineapple.

Metro-tini

6 parts Vodka
3 parts Orange Liqueur
2 parts Cranberry Juice
1 splash Lime Juice

Pour ingredients into a shaker with cracked ice and shake well. Strain into chilled martini glasses. Garnish with a lime wedge.

Monkey Business

3 parts Cranberry Vodka
2 parts Havana Club
1 part Pineapple Juice

Pour ingredients into a shaker with cracked ice and shake well. Strain into chilled martini glasses. Garnish with fresh coconut.

Nancy Boy

4 parts Vodka
1 part Triple Sec
1 part Cranberry Juice
1 splash Lime Juice
1 drop Grenadine

Pour all ingredients except Grenadine into a shaker with cracked ice and shake well. Strain into chilled martini glasses. Add a drop of Grenadine to finish. Garnish with an orange slice.

Nickel Martini

2 parts Currant Vodka
1 part Triple Sec
1 part Orange Juice

Pour ingredients into a shaker with cracked ice and shake well. Strain into chilled martini glasses. Garnish with an orange twist.

Noon Ease Martini

16 parts Gin
1 part Extra Dry Vermouth
1 part Cranberry Juice
1 part Grapefruit Juice

Pour ingredients into a shaker with cracked ice and shake well. Strain into chilled martini glasses. Garnish with a lemon twist.

O Martini

4 parts Orange Vodka
2 parts Orange Liqueur
2 parts Orange Juice

Pour ingredients into a shaker with cracked ice and shake well. Strain into chilled martini glasses. Garnish with an orange wedge.

Orange Crush

3 parts Orange Vodka
1 part Orange Liqueur
1 splash Orange juice

Pour ingredients into a shaker with cracked ice and shake well. Strain into chilled martini glasses. Garnish with an orange twist.

Orange Fool

1 part Vodka
1 part Mandarin Orange Juice
1 splash Sweet Red Vermouth

Pour ingredients into a shaker with cracked ice and shake well. Strain into chilled martini glasses.

Orange Martini

2 parts Vodka
1 part Orange Brandy

Pour ingredients into a shaker with cracked ice and shake well. Strain into chilled martini glasses. Garnish with an orange slice.

Orange Martini 2

6 parts Vodka
1 part Triple Sec
1 dash Bitters

Pour ingredients into a shaker with cracked ice and shake well. Strain into chilled martini glasses. Garnish with an orange twist.

Orange Martini 3

2 parts Orange Vodka
1 part Orange Liqueur

Pour ingredients into a shaker with cracked ice and shake well. Strain into chilled martini glasses. Garnish with an orange twist.

Paradigm Shift

4 parts Gin
8 parts Vodka
4 parts Raspberry Juice
4 parts Grapefruit Juice
1 part Lemon-Lime Juice
1 splash Campari

Begin with ice-cold martini glasses. Swirl the glasses with campari disposing of excess. Pour remaining ingredients into a shaker with cracked ice and shake well. Strain into chilled martini glasses. Garnish with frozen grapefruit wedges (peeled) and raspberries.

Passionate Martini

2 parts Vodka
5 parts Alize Red Passion Liqueur
1 part Cranberry Juice

Pour ingredients into a shaker with cracked ice and shake well. Strain into chilled martini glasses. Garnish with a lemon twist.

Peach Blossom Martini

6 parts Peach Vodka
1 part Dubonnet Rouge
1 part Maraschino Liqueur

Pour ingredients into a shaker with cracked ice and shake well. Strain into chilled martini glasses. Garnish with a peach slice.

Peach Kiss

5 parts Vodka
1 part Peach Schnapps

Pour ingredients into a shaker with cracked ice and shake well. Strain into chilled martini glasses. Garnish with an orange twist.

Peachie Keen Martini

5 parts Cranberry Vodka
1 part Peach Brandy

Pour ingredients into a shaker with cracked ice and shake well. Strain into chilled martini glasses. Garnish with an orange twist.

Peachy Martini

3 parts Strawberry Vodka
1 part Peach Brandy

Pour ingredients into a shaker with cracked ice and shake well. Strain into chilled martini glasses. Garnish with a strawberry.

Pear Martini

2 parts Vodka
1 part Pear Liqueur

Pour ingredients into a shaker with cracked ice and shake well. Strain into chilled martini glasses. Garnish with a fresh pear half.

Pineapple Rush Martini

4 parts Vodka
1 part Ginseng Juice
1 part Pineapple Juice

Pour ingredients into a shaker with cracked ice and shake well. Strain into chilled martini glasses. Garnish with a pineapple wedge.

Pink Daze Martini

10 parts Vodka
1 part Triple Sec
1 part Lemon Juice
Sugar Cubes

Place a sugar cube into chilled martini glasses and cover with Triple Sec. Pour remaining ingredients into a shaker with cracked ice and shake well. Strain into glasses. Garnish with a lemon wheel.

Pink Diamond Martini

3 parts Vodka
2 parts Pineapple Vodka
1 part Cranberry Vodka
1 part Peach Schnapps

Pour ingredients into a shaker with cracked ice and let stand for 3 minutes. Gently tip shaker back and forth a few times. Strain into chilled martini glasses. Garnish with a perfect cherry and float rose petals on top.

Planter's Punch Martini

4 parts Vodka
4 parts Amber Rum
2 parts Pineapple Juice
1 part Lime Juice

Pour ingredients into a shaker with cracked ice and shake well. Strain into chilled martini glasses. Garnish with a pineapple wedge.

Quarterdeck Martini

6 parts Berry Vodka
1 part Maraschino Liqueur
1 part Grapefruit Juice

Pour ingredients into a shaker with cracked ice and shake well. Strain into chilled martini glasses. Garnish with a sprig of fresh mint.

Raspberry Martini

3 parts Raspberry Vodka
1 part Triple Sec

Pour ingredients into a shaker with cracked ice and shake well. Strain into chilled martini glasses. Garnish with raspberries.

Raspberry Cooler Martini

2 parts Vodka
1 part Raspberry Liqueur
2 parts Pink Lemonade

Pour ingredients into a shaker with cracked ice and shake well. Strain into chilled martini glasses. Garnish with raspberries.

Raspcinsational

2 parts Raspberry Liqueur
1 part Raspberry Vodka
1 part Cinnamon Liqueur

Pour ingredients into a shaker with cracked ice and shake well. Strain into chilled martini glasses. Garnish with fresh raspberries.

Razzbutini

4 parts Raspberry Vodka
1 part Raspberry Liqueur

Rim martini glasses with sugar. Pour ingredients into a shaker with cracked ice and shake well. Strain into chilled martini glasses. Garnish with raspberries.

Razz Ma Tazz

3 parts Raspberry Vodka
2 parts Cranberry Juice
1 splash Lime Juice

Pour ingredients into a shaker with cracked ice and shake well. Strain into chilled martini glasses. Garnish with a lime twist.

Razz Mania

3 parts Raspberry Vodka
1 part Raspberry Juice
1 part Triple Sec
1 dash Sour Mix

Pour ingredients into a shaker with cracked ice and shake well. Strain into chilled martini glasses. Garnish with raspberries.

Red Apple Martini

1 part Vodka
1 part Sour Apple Schnapps
1 part Cranberry Juice

Pour ingredients into a shaker with cracked ice and shake well. Strain into chilled martini glasses. Garnish with a thin apple slice.

Red Delicious Martini

3 parts Vodka
1 splash Italian Aperitif
1 splash Sour Apple Schnapps
2 parts Cranberry Juice

Pour ingredients into a shaker with cracked ice and shake well. Strain into chilled martini glasses. Garnish with an apple wedge. This drink should smell like a red delicious apple.

Resolution Martini

6 parts Peach Vodka
2 parts Apricot Brandy
1 part Lemon Juice

Pour ingredients into a shaker with cracked ice and shake well. Strain into chilled martini glasses. Garnish with a lemon twist.

Ruby Slipper

1 part Cranberry Vodka
1 part Triple Sec
1 part Sloe Gin
1 splash Sour Mix
1 splash Cranberry Juice

Pour ingredients into a shaker with cracked ice and shake well. Strain into chilled martini glasses. Garnish with an orange twist.

Rum Crantini

8 parts Lemon Rum
1 splash Cranberry Juice
1 dash Extra Dry Vermouth

Pour ingredients into a shaker with cracked ice and shake well. Strain into chilled martini glasses. Garnish with cranberries and a lemon twist.

St. Bernard

5 parts Vodka
2 parts Ruby Red Grapefruit Juice
1 part Peach Vodka

Pour ingredients into a shaker with cracked ice and shake well. Strain into chilled martini glasses. Garnish with a slice of ruby red grapefruit.

Seventh Heaven

6 parts Gin
1 part Maraschino Liqueur
1 part Grapefruit Juice

Pour ingredients into a shaker with cracked ice and shake well. Strain into chilled martini glasses. Garnish with a sprig of fresh mint.

Sex & Violets

3 parts Gin
1 part Parfait Armour

Pour ingredients into a shaker with cracked ice and shake well. Strain into chilled martini glasses. Garnish with an orange twist and for extra effect float violets on surface of drink.

Silk Panty

1 part Vodka
1 part Peach Schnapps
1 part Cranberry Juice

Pour ingredients into a shaker with cracked ice and shake well. Strain into chilled martini glasses. Garnish with a fresh peach slice.

Skip Smooth Martini

4 parts Vodka
2 parts Peach Schnapps
2 parts Orange Liqueur
1 part Grenadine Syrup

Pour ingredients into a shaker with cracked ice and shake well. Strain into chilled martini glasses. Garnish with a lime twist.

Stiff Breeze

4 parts Vodka
2 parts Grapefruit Juice
1 part Lime Juice
1 part Cranberry Juice Concentrate

Pour all ingredients except Cranberry Concentrate into a shaker with cracked ice and shake well. Strain into chilled martini glasses. Slowly pour concentrate down side of glass to create layers.

Strawberry Blonde

3 parts Strawberry Vodka
1 part Lillet Blanc

Pour ingredients into a shaker with cracked ice and shake well. Strain into chilled martini glasses. Garnish with a strawberry.

Strawberry Martini

1 part Vodka or Gin
1 part Strawberry Schnapps

Pour ingredients into a shaker with cracked ice and shake well. Strain into chilled martini glasses. Garnish with a strawberry.

Summer Breeze Martini

6 parts Citrus Vodka
2 parts Melon Liqueur
1 part Dry Vermouth
1 splash Lemon Juice

Pour ingredients into a shaker with cracked ice and shake well. Strain into chilled martini glasses. Garnish with honeydew melon balls.

Sunset Martini

6 parts Vodka
1 part Coconut Rum
12 parts Pineapple Juice
1 part Coconut Syrup
1 dash Grenadine

Pour all ingredients except Grenadine into a shaker with cracked ice and shake well. Strain into chilled martini glasses. Add a dash of Grenadine to each glass and garnish with a pineapple wedge.

Surfer Martini

6 parts Vodka
2 parts Coconut Rum
1 part Banana Liqueur

Pour ingredients into a shaker with cracked ice and shake well.
Strain into chilled martini glasses. Garnish with a pineapple wedge.

Tangerine Martini

1 part Vodka or Gin
1 part Tangerine Liqueur or Tangerine Juice

Pour ingredients into a shaker with cracked ice and shake well.
Strain into chilled martini glasses. Garnish with a frozen tangerine
wedge.

Tangertini

3 parts Vodka
1 part Lime Juice
1 part Tangerine Liqueur or Tangerine Juice

Pour ingredients into a shaker with cracked ice and shake well.
Strain into chilled martini glasses. Garnish with a frozen tangerine
wedge.

The Balaclava

2 parts Cranberry Vodka
1 part Raspberry Liqueur
1 part Gin
1 part Triple Sec

Pour ingredients into a shaker with cracked ice and shake well.
Strain into chilled martini glasses.

Top Banana Martini

8 parts Vodka
3 parts Banana Liqueur
4 parts Cranberry Juice

Pour ingredients into a shaker with cracked ice and shake well.
Strain into chilled martini glasses. Garnish with banana slices. *Hint:
to keep banana slices from browning, toss with fresh lemon juice and
keep chilled.*

Triggertini

2 parts Pineapple Vodka
2 parts Strawberry Vodka
1 part Raspberry Liqueur
1 part Triple Sec
1 part Cranberry Juice
1 part Lemonade

Pour ingredients into a shaker with cracked ice and shake well. Strain into chilled martini glasses. Garnish with an orange twist.

Triple Citrus Martini

2 parts Lemon Vodka
1 part Lime Juice
1 part Triple Sec

Pour ingredients into a shaker with cracked ice and shake well. Strain into chilled martini glasses. Garnish with a lemon twist.

Tropical Martini

5 parts Alize Red Passion Liqueur
1 part Coconut Rum

Pour ingredients into a shaker with cracked ice and shake well. Strain into chilled martini glasses. Garnish with a maraschino cherry.

Twisted Napoleon

3 parts Citrus Vodka
1 part Orange Brandy
1 part Lime Juice
2 parts Cranberry Juice

Pour ingredients into a shaker with cracked ice and shake well. Strain into chilled martini glasses. Garnish with orange and lemon twists.

Ultimate Cranberry Martini

4 parts Vodka
1 part Triple Sec
1 part Cranberry Juice

Fill glasses with ice. Pour ingredients into a shaker with cracked ice and shake well. Strain into chilled martini glasses. Garnish with a lime twist.

Ultraviolet

1 part Vodka
1 part Orange Liqueur
3 parts Cranberry Juice
1 splash Pineapple Juice

Pour ingredients into a shaker with cracked ice and shake well. Strain into chilled martini glasses. Garnish with a lemon slice and fresh blueberries.

Very Peachy Martini

1 part Peach Vodka
1 part Peach Schnapps
1 part Peach Juice

Pour ingredients into a shaker with cracked ice and shake well. Strain into chilled martini glasses. Garnish with a canned peach slice.

Voo Doo Doll

3 parts Vodka
2 parts Raspberry Liqueur
1 part Cranberry Juice
1 squeeze of Lemon Juice

Pour ingredients into a shaker with cracked ice and shake well. Strain into chilled martini glasses. Garnish with a lime twist.

Watermelon Martini

12 parts Vodka
1 part Triple Sec
1 part Watermelon Liqueur

Pour ingredients into a shaker with cracked ice and shake well. Strain into chilled martini glasses. Garnish with a watermelon wedge. *Hint: Remove seeds from watermelon.*

Watermelontini

3 parts Vodka
1 part Sour Watermelon Schnapps

Rim martini glasses with sugar. Pour ingredients into a shaker with cracked ice and shake well. Strain into chilled martini glasses. Garnish a with watermelon wedge. *Hint: Remove seeds from watermelon.*

Woo Woo Martini

6 parts Cranberry Vodka
1 part Peach Schnapps

Pour ingredients into a shaker with cracked ice and shake well. Strain into chilled martini glasses. Garnish with a lemon twist.

Woo Woo Too

3 parts Black Vodka
1 part Peach Schnapps
1 dash Cranberry Juice
1 splash Triple Sec

Wipe rims of martini glasses with fresh orange zest. Pour ingredients into a shaker with cracked ice and let stand for 3 minutes. Strain into chilled martini glasses. Garnish with cranberries and strawberries. *Hint: never shake this martini, it will end up like a smoothy - you may enjoy it this way as well though.*

THE TRENDY MARTINIS

"You can no more keep a Martini in the refrigerator than you can keep a kiss there. The proper union of gin and vermouth is... one of the happiest marriages on earth, and one of the shortest lived."

— Bernard DeVoto —

24 Karats

2 parts Amaretto
2 parts Raspberry Liqueur
1 part Vanilla Vodka
1 splash Orange Juice
1 splash Lime Cordial

Pour ingredients into a shaker with cracked ice and shake well. Strain into chilled martini glasses. Garnish with an orange twist.

4th of July Martini

1 part Jack Daniels
1 part Triple Sec
1 part Sweet & Sour Mix
4 parts lemon-lime soda

Pour ingredients into a shaker with cracked ice and shake well. Strain into chilled martini glasses. Garnish with a lemon wedge.

Absinthe Minded

6 parts Vodka
3 parts Absinthe
2 parts Cranberry Juice
1 part Blue Curaçao

Pour ingredients into a shaker with cracked ice and shake well. Strain into chilled martini glasses. Garnish with an orange wedge.

Absolute Martini

5 parts Vodka
1 part Triple Sec
2 parts Lemon Juice
1 dash Bitters

Pour ingredients into a shaker with cracked ice and shake well. Strain into chilled martini glasses. Garnish with a lemon twist.

After The Frost

1 part Gin
1 part Ice Wine
1 splash Calvados

Pour ingredients into a shaker with cracked ice and shake well. Strain into chilled martini glasses. Garnish with frozen grapes.

Air Gunner Martini

3 parts Vodka
1 part Lemon Liqueur
Drop of Blue Curaçao

Pour ingredients into a shaker with cracked ice and shake well. Strain into chilled martini glasses. Garnish with a lemon twist.

Alabama Martini

4 parts Vodka
4 parts Orange Juice
1 part Whiskey
1 part Lemon Liqueur

Pour ingredients into a shaker with cracked ice and shake well. Strain into chilled martini glasses. Garnish with an orange slice.

Algonquin Martini

4 parts Vodka
4 parts Rye
3 parts Dry Vermouth
3 parts Pineapple Juice

Pour ingredients into a shaker with cracked ice and shake well. Strain into chilled martini glasses. Garnish with a cherry.

Allen Martini

4 parts Gin
1 part Maraschino Liqueur
1 part Lemon Juice

Pour ingredients into a shaker with cracked ice and shake well. Strain into chilled martini glasses. Garnish with a lemon twist.

Anti-Freeze Martini

6 parts Vodka
2 parts Blue Curaçao
2 parts Midori Melon Liqueur
1 part Pineapple Juice

Pour ingredients into a shaker with cracked ice and shake well. Strain into chilled martini glasses. Garnish with a lemon twist.

Aperitivo Martini

2 parts Gin
1 part White Sambuca
5 dashes Bitters

Pour ingredients into a shaker with cracked ice and shake well. Strain into chilled martini glasses. Garnish with an orange peel.

Armada Martini

3 parts Vodka
1 part Amontillado Sherry

Pour ingredients into a shaker with cracked ice and shake well.
Strain into chilled martini glasses. Garnish with an orange twist.

Aviation Martini

6 parts Gin
4 parts Lemon Juice
1 part Cherry Liqueur

Pour ingredients into a shaker with cracked ice and shake well.
Strain into chilled martini glasses. Garnish with a cherry.

Aviation Citron Martini

6 parts Citron Vodka
4 parts Lemon Juice
1 part Cherry Liqueur

Pour ingredients into a shaker with cracked ice and shake well.
Strain into chilled martini glasses. Garnish with a cherry.

Bacardi Limon Martini

4 parts Bacardi Limon Rum
1 part Cranberry Juice
1 dash Dry Vermouth.

Pour ingredients into a shaker with cracked ice and shake well.
Strain into chilled cocktail glasses. Garnish with a lemon wedge.

Bacardi Martini

6 parts White Rum
1 part Dry Vermouth

Pour ingredients into a shaker with cracked ice and shake well.
Strain into chilled martini glasses. Garnish with an olive.

Balalajka Martini

5 parts Vodka or Gin
1 part Orange Juice

Pour ingredients into a shaker with cracked ice and shake well.
Strain into chilled martini glasses. Garnish with an orange twist.

Barbed Wire

8 parts Vodka
2 parts Sweet Vermouth
1 part Pernod
1 part Raspberry Liqueur

Pour ingredients into a shaker with cracked ice and shake well. Strain into chilled martini glasses. Garnish with a lemon twist.

Bedlestone

2 parts Scotch
1 part Dry Vermouth

Pour ingredients into a shaker with cracked ice and shake well. Strain into chilled martini glasses. Garnish with a lemon twist.

Bee's Kiss Martini

2 parts Vodka
4 parts White Rum
1 part Dark Rum
3 parts Cream
2 tsp Honey

Pour all ingredients except honey into a shaker with cracked ice and shake well. Strain into chilled martini glasses. Drizzle honey into each glass and sprinkle with ground nutmeg.

Bellini Martini

2 parts Vodka
1 part Peach Schnapps
1 part Champagne

Pour all ingredients except champagne into a shaker with cracked ice and shake well. Strain into chilled martini glasses. Top each glass with champagne and garnish with raspberries.

Between the Sheets

1 part Brandy
1 part Cointreau
1 part Light Rum
1 splash Lemon Juice

Pour ingredients into a shaker with cracked ice and shake well. Strain into chilled martini glasses. Garnish with an orange wedge.

Bikini Martini

2 parts Vodka
1 part Coconut Rum
1 splash Grenadine Syrup

Pour all ingredients except Grenadine into a shaker with cracked ice and shake well. Strain into chilled martini glasses. Slowly drizzle Grenadine into each glass. Garnish with an orange wedge.

Bikini Martini 2

4 parts Vodka
2 parts Light Rum
1 part Cream
2 parts Lemon Juice
2 tsp Bar Sugar

Pour ingredients into a shaker with cracked ice and shake well. Strain into chilled martini glasses. Garnish with a lemon twist.

Black & White Martini

2 parts Vanilla Vodka
1 part Crème de Cacao

Pour ingredients into a shaker with cracked ice and shake well. Strain into chilled martini glasses. Garnish with black & white licorice candies.

Black Bucca Martini

2 parts Vodka
1 part Black Sambuca

Pour ingredients into a shaker with cracked ice and shake well. Strain into chilled martini glasses. Garnish with black licorice or a chocolate covered coffee bean.

Black Cat Martini

1 part Black Vodka
1 part Chambord

Pour ingredients into a shaker with cracked ice and shake well. Strain into chilled martini glasses.

Black Dog Martini

6 parts Light Rum
1 part Dry Vermouth

Pour ingredients into a shaker with cracked ice and shake well. Strain into chilled martini glasses. Garnish with a black olive.

Black Ice Martini

4 parts Vodka
4 parts Black Sambuca
1 part Crème de Menthe

Pour ingredients into a shaker with cracked ice and shake well. Strain into chilled martini glasses.

Black on Black Martini

16 parts Black Vodka
1 part Black Sambuca

Pour ingredients into a shaker with cracked ice and shake well. Strain into chilled martini glasses. Garnish with a licorice stick.

Black Russian Martini

5 parts Vodka
1 part Kahlua

Pour ingredients into a shaker with cracked ice and shake well. Strain into chilled martini glasses.

Bloodhound Martini

2 parts Gin
1 part Dry Vermouth
1 part Sweet Vermouth
1 part Strawberry Liqueur

Pour ingredients into a shaker with cracked ice and shake well. Strain into chilled martini glasses. Garnish with a large fresh strawberry.

Bloody Martini

3 parts Pepper Vodka
3 parts Citron Vodka
1 part Bloody Mary Mix

Rim chilled glasses with celery salt. Pour ingredients into a shaker with cracked ice and shake well. Strain into chilled martini glasses. Garnish with a lemon twist.

Blue Collar Martini

1 part Vodka
1 part Beer

Pour vodka into chilled martini glasses, top with cold beer. Garnish with a lemon twist.

Boardwalk Martini

12 parts Vodka
4 parts Dry Vermouth
1 part Maraschino Liqueur
2 parts Lemon Juice

Pour ingredients into a shaker with cracked ice and shake well. Strain into chilled martini glasses. Garnish with a lemon twist.

Boomerang Martini

3 parts Gin
1 part Dry Vermouth
1 dash Bitters
1 dash Maraschino Liqueur

Pour ingredients into a shaker with cracked ice and shake well. Strain into chilled martini glasses. Garnish with a kiwi slice.

Bootlegger Martini

8 parts Gin
1 part Southern Comfort

Stir ingredients gently with ice and strain into a chilled martini glass. Garnish with a lemon twist.

Brazen Martini

3 parts Vodka
1 part Triple Sec

Pour ingredients into a shaker with cracked ice and shake well. Strain into chilled martini glasses. Garnish with an orange twist.

Broadway Martini

6 parts Gin
1 part White Crème de Menthe

Pour ingredients into a shaker with cracked ice and shake well. Strain into chilled martini glasses. Garnish with a fresh sprig of mint.

Bronx Martini

6 parts Gin
1 part Orange Juice
1 squeeze of Lemon Juice

Pour ingredients into a shaker with cracked ice and shake well. Strain into chilled martini glasses. Garnish with a lemon twist.

Bronx Martini 2

2 parts Gin
1 part Dry Vermouth
1 part Sweet Vermouth
2 parts Orange Juice

Pour ingredients into a shaker with cracked ice and shake well. Strain into chilled martini glasses. Garnish with an orange twist.

Bronx Terrace Martini

6 parts Gin
2 parts Lime Juice
1 part Dry Vermouth

Pour ingredients into a shaker with cracked ice and shake well. Strain into chilled martini glasses. Garnish with a cherry.

Brown Martini

4 parts Gin
2 parts Light Rum
1 part Dry Vermouth

Pour ingredients into a shaker with cracked ice and shake well. Strain into chilled martini glasses. Garnish with a kumquat.

Bubbly Martini

1 part Chilled Vodka
1 part Chilled Champagne

Pour vodka into chilled martini glasses and top with champagne. Garnish with a frozen strawberry.

Buckly Martini

5 parts Vodka
1 part Frangelico Hazelnut Liqueur

Pour ingredients into a shaker with cracked ice and shake well. Strain into chilled martini glasses.

Burnt Orange Martini

8 parts Vodka
1 part Bourbon
1 part Triple Sec
151 Proof Rum

Prior to mixing, prepare orange twist by soaking in 151 Proof rum. Pour ingredients into a shaker with cracked ice and shake well. Strain into chilled martini glasses. Remove soaked orange twists and place into a fire proof dish and light on fire. Let twists burn until slightly charred. Garnish martinis with them.

Busy Bee Sting Martini

2 parts Vodka
4 parts Brandy
2 parts Crème de Menthe
1 part Honey Liqueur

Pour ingredients into a shaker with cracked ice and shake well. Strain into chilled martini glasses. Garnish with a fresh mint sprig.

CC Bellini

4 parts Champagne
1 part Vodka
1 part Chambord

Pour Champagne into chilled martini glasses. Pour remaining ingredients into a shaker with cracked ice and shake well. Strain into prepared glasses. Drop a frozen raspberry into centre of glass.

Cabaret Martini

2 parts Gin
1 part Dubonnet Rouge
5 dashes Bitters
8 dashes Pernod

Pour ingredients into a shaker with cracked ice and shake well. Strain into chilled martini glasses. Garnish with a lime twist.

Cajun Martini

2 parts Inferno Vodka
1 part Dry Vermouth

Pour ingredients into a shaker with cracked ice and shake well. Strain into chilled martini glasses. Garnish with an olive and a chili pepper.

Campari Martini

6 parts Vodka
1 part Campari

Pour ingredients into a shaker with cracked ice and shake well. Strain into chilled martini glasses. Garnish with a lime twist.

Captain Morgan's Revenge

4 parts Spiced Rum
1 part Cranberry Juice
1 dash Dry Vermouth

Pour ingredients into a shaker with cracked ice and shake well. Strain into chilled martini glasses. Garnish with a lemon twist.

Caribou Martini

4 parts Chilled Coffee Vodka
1 part Chilled Champagne

Pour vodka into chilled martini glasses. Top with champagne and stir gently. Garnish with a lemon twist and a coffee bean.

Cellatini

8 parts Vodka
1 part Lemoncella

Pour ingredients into a shaker with cracked ice and shake well. Strain into chilled martini glasses. Garnish with a lemon wheel and a whole fresh strawberry or add your favourite berries.

Chartini

5 parts Vodka
1 part Green Chartreuse

Pour ingredients into a shaker with cracked ice and shake well. Strain into chilled martini glasses. Garnish with a lemon twist.

Cinnamon Limeade Martini

2 parts Vodka
1 part Cinnamon Schnapps
2 parts Frozen Limeade

Pour ingredients into a shaker with cracked ice and shake well. Strain into chilled martini glasses. Garnish with a lime wedge.

Cirrus

2 parts Vanilla Vodka
1 part Orange Liqueur

Pour ingredients into a shaker with cracked ice and shake well. Strain into chilled martini glasses. Garnish with an orange twist.

Clear-Coin Martini

1 part Vodka
1 part Campari
2 parts Orange Juice

Rinse chilled martini glasses with Campari. Pour remaining ingredients into a shaker with cracked ice and shake well. Strain into chilled martini glasses. Garnish with an orange twist.

Clover Club Martini

6 parts Gin or Vodka
3 parts Lemon Juice
1 part Grenadine

Pour ingredients into a shaker with cracked ice and shake well. Strain into chilled martini glasses. Garnish with a lemon twist.

Cocaine Lady Martini

2 parts Vodka
1 part Amaretto
1 part Kahlua
1 part Bailey's

Pour ingredients into a shaker with cracked ice and shake well. Strain into chilled martini glasses. Garnish with shaved white chocolate.

Cocomelotini

2 parts Vodka
1 part Coconut Rum
1 part Melon Liqueur
1 splash Sour Mix

Pour ingredients into a shaker with cracked ice and shake well. Strain into chilled martini glasses. Garnish with a kiwi slice.

Coconut Grove

1 part Infused Vodka

To infuse vodka: Infuse 26 oz. of vodka with the meat of one coconut. Pour ingredients into a shaker with cracked ice and shake well. Strain into chilled martini glasses. Garnish with shaved coconut.

Coconutini

2 parts Vodka
1 part Coconut Rum

Pour ingredients into a shaker with cracked ice and shake well. Strain into chilled martini glasses. Garnish with shaved coconut.

Cold Comfort Martini

1 part Lemon Vodka
1 part Honey Vodka

Pour ingredients into a shaker with cracked ice and shake well. Strain into chilled martini glasses. Garnish with a lemon twist.

Comfortable Martini

6 parts Honey Vodka
1 part Southern Comfort

Pour ingredients into a shaker with cracked ice and shake well. Strain into chilled martini glasses. Garnish with a twist of orange.

Copper Martini

4 parts Gin
2 parts Triple Sec
1 part Campari

Pour ingredients into a shaker with cracked ice and shake well. Strain into chilled martini glasses. Garnish with a lemon twist.

Copper Illusion Martini

2 parts Gin
1 part Grand Marnier
1 part Campari

Pour ingredients into a shaker with cracked ice and shake well. Strain into chilled martini glasses. Garnish with an orange slice.

Coppertone Tan Martini

2 parts Light Rum
2 parts Amaretto

Pour ingredients into a shaker with cracked ice and shake well. Strain into chilled martini glasses. Garnish with an orange twist.

Courvoisier-tini

2 parts Vodka
1 part Cognac

Pour ingredients into a shaker with cracked ice and shake well. Strain into chilled martini glasses. Garnish with a lemon twist.

Crabshack-tini

7 parts Vodka
3 parts Tequila
2 parts Tomato Clam Juice

In the bottom of chilled martini glasses place a cooked crab claw and a dollop of horseradish. Pour ingredients into a shaker with cracked ice and shake well. Strain into the prepared martini glasses. Dust with salt and pepper and garnish with an olive.

Creole Martini

8 parts Inferno Vodka
1 part Bloody Mary Mix

Pour ingredients into a shaker with cracked ice and shake well. Strain into chilled martini glasses. Garnish with a chili pepper.

Crimson Martini

8 part Gin
2 parts Ruby Port
2 parts Triple Sec
1 dash Grenadine

Pour all ingredients except Grenadine into a shaker with cracked ice and shake well. Strain into chilled martini glasses. Put a dash of Grenadine into each glass and garnish with a lime twist.

Damsel in Distress

2 parts Lemon Vodka
1 part Coconut Rum
1 splash Orange Juice
1 splash Sour Mix
1 splash Scotch

Pour a splash of Scotch into chilled martini glasses. Pour remaining ingredients into a shaker with cracked ice and shake well. Strain into prepared martini glasses.

Davis Martini

3 parts Dark Rum
3 parts Dry Vermouth
2 parts Lime Juice
1 dash of Grenadine

Pour ingredients into a shaker with cracked ice and shake well. Strain into chilled martini glasses. Garnish with a lime twist.

Daydream Martini

6 parts Citrus Vodka
1 part Triple Sec
2 parts Orange Juice
1 dash of Bar Sugar (to taste)

Pour ingredients into a shaker with cracked ice and shake well. Strain into chilled martini glasses. Garnish with an orange wedge.

Desert Cactus Martilla

6 parts Tequila
2 parts Metaxa Ouzo
2 parts Mezcal
1 part Melon Liqueur
1 splash Cranberry Juice

Pour ingredients into a shaker with cracked ice and shake well. Strain into chilled martini glasses. Garnish with a lime twist.

Desperate Martini

6 parts Gin
1 part Dry Vermouth
1 part Black Berry Brandy

Pour ingredients into a shaker with cracked ice and shake well. Strain into chilled martini glasses. Garnish with fresh blackberries.

Desperation Martini

3 parts Raspberry Vodka
1 part Chambord
1 part Cranberry Juice

Pour ingredients into a shaker with cracked ice and shake well. Strain into chilled martini glasses. Garnish with fresh raspberries.

Diego Martini

8 parts Vodka
1 part Tequila
1 part Orange Juice

Pour ingredients into a shaker with cracked ice and shake well. Strain into chilled martini glasses. Garnish with an orange wedge.

Dixie Dew

3 parts Bourbon
1 part Crème de Menthe
1 splash of Triple Sec

Pour ingredients into a shaker with cracked ice and shake well. Strain into chilled martini glasses. Garnish with an orange twist.

Dixie Stinger

6 parts Bourbon
1 part Peach Schnapps
1 part Champagne
1 splash of Southern Comfort

Pour all ingredients except champagne into a shaker with cracked ice and shake well. Strain into chilled martini glasses. Top each glass with champagne. Garnish with a peach slice.

Double Vision Martini

8 parts Vodka
3 parts Triple Sec
1 part Pineapple Juice

Pour ingredients into a shaker with cracked ice and shake well.
Strain into chilled martini glasses. Garnish with a pineapple wedge.

Dramtini

2 parts Drambuie
2 parts Vodka
1 splash of Dry Vermouth

Pour all ingredients except Vermouth into a shaker with cracked ice
and shake well. Strain into chilled martini glasses. Put a splash of
Vermouth into each glass and garnish with a cherry.

Eager Beaver Martini

3 parts Vodka
3 parts Kahlua
1 part Triple Sec

Pour ingredients into a shaker with cracked ice and shake well.
Strain into chilled martini glasses. Garnish with an orange twist.

East Wing Martini

6 parts Vodka
1 part Campari
2 parts Cherry Brandy

Pour ingredients into a shaker with cracked ice and shake well.
Strain into chilled martini glasses. Garnish with a lemon twist.

Eat My Martini

6 parts Honey Vodka
1 part Amontillado Sherry

Pour ingredients into a shaker with cracked ice and shake well.
Strain into chilled martini glasses. Garnish with a cherry.

El Diablo Martini

8 parts Tequila
3 parts Crème de Cassis
2 parts Lime Juice

Pour ingredients into a shaker with cracked ice and shake well.
Strain into chilled martini glasses. Garnish with a lime twist.

El Floridita Martini

4 parts Vodka
4 parts White Rum
2 parts Lime Juice
2 parts Sweet Vermouth
1 part White Crème de Cacao

Pour ingredients into a shaker with cracked ice and shake well. Strain into chilled martini glasses. Garnish with a lime twist.

Espionage Martini

8 parts Citrus Vodka
1 part Crème de Menthe

Pour ingredients into a shaker with cracked ice and shake well. Strain into chilled martini glasses. Garnish with a lemon twist.

Espionage Martini 2

6 parts Lemon Vodka
1 part Crème de Menthe

Pour ingredients into a shaker with cracked ice and shake well. Strain into chilled martini glasses. Garnish with a lemon twist.

Exterminator Martini

4 parts Vodka or Gin
1 part Fino Sherry

Pour ingredients into a shaker with cracked ice and shake well. Strain into chilled martini glasses. Garnish with a lemon twist.

Eye of the Storm

2 parts Currant Vodka
1 part Coconut Milk

Pour ingredients into a shaker with cracked ice and shake well. Strain into chilled martini glasses. Garnish with sliced strawberries.

Faster Pussycat

3 parts Vodka
2 parts Sour Mix
1 part Lime Juice

Pour ingredients into a shaker with cracked ice and shake well. Strain into chilled martini glasses. Garnish with a floating lime slice topped with a cherry.

Fine & Dandy Martini

2 parts Gin
1 part Triple Sec
1 part Lemon Juice
1 dash of bitters

Pour ingredients into a shaker with cracked ice and shake well.
Strain into chilled martini glasses. Garnish with a lemon twist.

Flirtini

1 part Raspberry Vodka
1 part Orange Liqueur
1 splash Lime Juice
1 splash Pineapple Juice
1 splash Cranberry Juice
1 part Brut Champagne

Muddle a few fresh raspberries in the bottom of chilled martini
glasses. Pour all ingredients except Champagne into a shaker with
cracked ice and shake well. Strain into prepared martini glasses.
Top with Champagne. Garnish with a fresh sprig of mint.

Floof

2 parts Raspberry Vodka
3 parts Champagne
1 part Chambord

Pour Vodka and Chambord into a shaker with cracked ice and
shake well. Strain into chilled martini glasses. Top with Champagne.
Garnish with a frozen raspberry.

Flying Dutchman Martini

8 parts Gin
1 part Dry Vermouth
1 part Blue Curaçao

Pour ingredients into a shaker with cracked ice and shake well.
Strain into chilled martini glasses. Garnish with a lemon twist.

Flying Dutchman Martini 2

3 parts Gin
1 part Dry Vermouth
1 part Blue Curaçao

Pour ingredients into a shaker with cracked ice and shake well.
Strain into chilled martini glasses. Garnish with a lemon twist.

French Kiss Martini

8 parts Orange Vodka
1 part Lillet

Pour ingredients into a shaker with cracked ice and shake well. Strain into chilled martini glasses.

French Kiss Martini 2

2 parts Vodka
1 part Raspberry Liqueur
1 part Pineapple Juice

Pour ingredients into a shaker with cracked ice and shake well. Strain into chilled martini glasses.

Frescatini

5 parts Gin
1 part Fresca
1 splash Cherry Juice

Rinse chilled martini glass with cherry juice. Pour in Gin. Top with Fresca. Garnish with a fresh Bing cherry.

Fretful Martini

6 parts Gin
1 part Blue Curaçao
1 dash of Bitters

Pour ingredients into a shaker with cracked ice and shake well. Strain into chilled martini glasses. Garnish with an olive.

Fuzzy Navel Lint

6 parts Vodka
2 parts Dry Vermouth
1 part Amaretto
1 part Orange Juice

Pour ingredients into a shaker with cracked ice and shake well. Strain into chilled martini glasses. Garnish with an orange wedge.

Gold Dust Martini

4 parts Vodka
1 part White Crème de Cacao
2 parts Goldschläger

Pour Vodka and Crème de Menthe into a shaker with cracked ice and shake well. Strain into chilled martini glasses. Top glasses with Goldschläger.

Golden Eye Martini

2 parts Vodka
1 part Cognac
1 part Amaretto Liqueur

Pour ingredients into a shaker with cracked ice and shake well.
Strain into chilled martini glasses. Garnish with an orange twist.

Golden Inferno Martini

1 part Inferno Vodka
1 part Goldschläger

Pour ingredients into a shaker with cracked ice and shake well.
Strain into chilled martini glasses. Garnish with a chili pepper.

Golden Temple

6 parts Vodka
1 part Punt e Mes

Pour ingredients into a shaker with cracked ice and shake well.
Strain into chilled martini glasses.

Goldschläger Martini

2 parts Vodka
1 part Goldschläger

Pour ingredients into a shaker with cracked ice and shake well.
Strain into chilled martini glasses. Garnish with a cinnamon stick.

Good Old Boys Martini

2 parts Vodka
1 part Bourbon

Pour ingredients into a shaker with cracked ice and shake well.
Strain into chilled martini glasses. Garnish with a lemon twist.

Grape Kool Aid

1 part Currant Vodka
1 splash Chambord
1 splash Lime Juice

Pour ingredients into a shaker with cracked ice and shake well.
Strain into chilled martini glasses.

Grasshopper Martini

6 parts Vodka
5 parts Crème de Cacao
1 part Crème de Menthe

Pour ingredients into a shaker with cracked ice and shake well. Strain into chilled martini glasses.

Green Goddess

3 parts Gin
1 part Green Chartreuse

Pour ingredients into a shaker with cracked ice and shake well. Strain into chilled martini glasses. Garnish with a lemon twist.

Green Machine

4 parts Gin or Vodka
3 parts Midori Melon Liqueur
1 splash Crème de Menthe
1 part Sweet Vermouth

Pour Sweet Vermouth into chilled martini glasses. Swirl to coat glasses and toss out excess. Pour remaining ingredients into a shaker with cracked ice and shake well. Strain into prepared glasses. Garnish with a daisy.

Green Martini

6 parts Gin
1 part Green Chartreuse

Pour ingredients into a shaker with cracked ice and shake well. Strain into chilled martini glasses. Garnish with an almond stuffed olive.

Groovy Martini

8 parts Vodka
4 parts Triple Sec
8 parts Cranberry Juice
1 part Crème de Cassis

Pour ingredients into a shaker with cracked ice and shake well. Strain into chilled martini glasses. Garnish with an orange wedge and cranberries.

Haemorrhaging Brain Martini

3 parts Vodka
2 parts Peach Schnapps
2 parts Bailey's
1 part Grenadine

Pour vodka and schnapps into a shaker with cracked ice and shake well. Strain into chilled martini glasses. Drizzle in Bailey's (the brain) and Grenadine (the haemorrhage).

Hair Raiser Martini

1 part Brandy
1 part Anisette
1 part Triple Sec

Pour ingredients into a shaker with cracked ice and shake well. Strain into chilled martini glasses.

Head Shrinker Martini

4 parts Gin
1 part Green Curaçao
2 parts Lemon Juice

Pour ingredients into a shaker with cracked ice and shake well. Strain into chilled martini glasses. Garnish with a lemon twist.

Hip Cat Martini

6 parts Berry Vodka
1 part Dry Vermouth
1 part Sweet Vermouth
1 dash Cointreau

Pour ingredients into a shaker with cracked ice and shake well. Strain into chilled martini glasses. Garnish with an orange twist.

Hollywood Martini

6 parts Vodka
1 part Goldwasser
1 part Dry Vermouth

Pour ingredients into a shaker with cracked ice and shake well. Strain into chilled martini glasses. Garnish with a blue cheese stuffed olive.

Holy Water

2 parts Vodka
1 part Blue Curaçao
1 part Red Sour Puss

Pour ingredients into a shaker with cracked ice and shake well. Strain into chilled martini glasses.

Hot & Dirty Martini

12 parts Pepper Vodka
2 parts Dry Vermouth
1 part Olive Brine

Pour ingredients into a shaker with cracked ice and shake well. Strain into chilled martini glasses. Garnish with a jalapeno stuffed olive.

Iceberg Martini 2

2 parts Gin
2 parts Currant Vodka
1 splash Sweet Vermouth

Coat inside of chilled martini glasses with sweet vermouth. Pour remaining ingredients into a shaker with cracked ice and shake well. Strain into prepared martini glasses. Garnish with a fresh sprig of mint.

Iceberg Martini 3

2 parts Gin
2 parts Currant Vodka
1 part Lemon Vodka
1 splash Crème de Menthe

Pour ingredients into a shaker with cracked ice and shake well. Strain into chilled martini glasses. Garnish with a fresh sprig of mint.

Ideal Martini

6 parts Gin
2 parts Dry Vermouth
1 part Maraschino Liqueur
1 tsp Lemon Juice

Pour ingredients into a shaker with cracked ice and shake well. Strain into chilled martini glasses. Garnish with a lemon twist.

Imperial Martini

6 parts Gin
2 parts Dry Vermouth
1 part Maraschino Liqueur
5 dashes Bitters

Pour ingredients into a shaker with cracked ice and shake well. Strain into chilled martini glasses. Garnish with a cherry.

Independence Day Martini

1 part Rye
2 parts Sherry
1 part Gingerale
1 splash Orange Juice

Pour all ingredients except Gingerale into a shaker with cracked ice and shake well. Strain into chilled martini glasses. Top with Gingerale. Garnish with an orange wedge.

Inferno Backdraft

1 part Inferno Vodka
1 part Harry's Hurricane Tropical Liqueur

Pour ingredients into a shaker with cracked ice and shake well. Strain into chilled martini glasses. Garnish with coconut.

Inferno Hot Chocolate

3 parts Inferno Vodka
1 part Crème de Cacao

Pour ingredients into a shaker with cracked ice and shake well. Strain into chilled martini glasses. Garnish with a chili pepper.

Island Martini

6 parts Gold Rum
1 part Dry Vermouth
1 part Sweet Vermouth

Pour ingredients into a shaker with cracked ice and shake well. Strain into chilled martini glasses. Garnish with a lemon twist.

Ivy Club Martini

3 parts Gin
1 part Amaretto
1 part Lime Juice

Pour ingredients into a shaker with cracked ice and shake well. Strain into chilled martini glasses. Garnish with a lime twist.

Jack-N-Chill

5 parts Vodka
1 part Jack Daniels

Pour ingredients into a shaker with cracked ice and shake well. Strain into chilled martini glasses. Garnish with three olives.

Jaguar Roartini

5 parts Lemon Vodka
2 parts Blue Curaçao
2 parts Sour Mix
1 part Triple Sec

Pour ingredients into a shaker with cracked ice and shake well. Strain into chilled martini glasses. Garnish with a cherry.

Jamaican Pine Nut

10 parts Dark Rum
10 parts Pineapple Juice
5 parts Amaretto
1 splash Dry Vermouth

Place a single salted almond into chilled martini glasses. Pour ingredients into a shaker with cracked ice and shake well. Strain into chilled martini glasses. Garnish with a pineapple wedge.

Jewel Martini

2 parts Gin
1 part Green Curaçao
1 part Dry Vermouth

Pour ingredients into a shaker with cracked ice and shake well. Strain into chilled martini glasses. Garnish with a lemon twist.

J.J. Jimmy Crack Corn... Who Cares?

1 part Jack Daniels
1 part Johnnie Walker Black Label Scotch
1 part Jim Bean Whiskey

Pour ingredients into a chilled glass pitcher with lots of ice. Beat ice until it screams. (If you listen you can really hear something). The key to this drink is that you break the ice up to the point where when poured there will be a layer of ice on top serve immediately, if it sits it's ruined.

Journalist Martini

8 parts Gin
1 part Dry Vermouth
1 part Sweet Vermouth
1 part Triple Sec
1 part Lime Juice
1 dash Bitters

Pour ingredients into a shaker with cracked ice and shake well. Strain into chilled martini glasses. Garnish with a lemon twist.

Lava Lamp Martini

10 parts Vodka
1 part Raspberry Liqueur
1 part Honey

Mix the liqueur with the honey in a shot glass. Pour vodka into a shaker with cracked ice and shake well. Strain into chilled martini glasses. Drizzle honey mixture into glasses.

Lazy Guy's Martini

3 parts Whiskey (or more)
1 splash Coca Cola

Pour Rye into a shaker with cracked ice and shake well. Strain into chilled martini glasses. Top with Coca Cola. Garnish with a lime twist.

Le Diamant

8 parts Vodka
1 part Balsamic Vinaigrette

Pour ingredients into a shaker with cracked ice and shake well. Strain into chilled martini glasses. Garnish with fresh tarragon.

Leap Year Martini

8 parts Gin or Vodka
2 parts Sweet Vermouth
2 parts Triple Sec
1 part Lemon Juice

Pour ingredients into a shaker with cracked ice and shake well. Strain into chilled martini glasses. Garnish with an orange twist.

Leap Year Martini 2

6 parts Citrus Vodka
1 part Sweet Vermouth
1 part Triple Sec
1 splash Lemon Juice

Pour ingredients into a shaker with cracked ice and shake well. Strain into chilled martini glasses. Garnish with an orange twist.

Lemon & Spice

3 parts Citron Vodka
3 parts Pepper Vodka
1 part Dry Vermouth

Pour ingredients into a shaker with cracked ice and shake well. Strain into chilled martini glasses. Garnish with a lemon twist.

Lemon Drop

1 part Frozen Vodka

Pour into chilled martini glasses. Garnish with a lemon wedge dipped in sugar.

Lemon Drop 2

3 parts Vodka
1 part Lemon Juice
1 tsp Sugar

Pour ingredients into a shaker with cracked ice and shake well. Strain into chilled martini glasses. Garnish with a lemon twist.

Lemon Drop 3

6 parts Citron Vodka
1 part Dry Vermouth

Rim chilled martini glasses with white sugar. Pour ingredients into a shaker with cracked ice and shake well. Strain into chilled martini glasses. Garnish with a lemon wheel.

Lemon Twist Martini

6 parts Lemon Rum
1 part Dry Vermouth

Pour ingredients into a shaker with cracked ice and shake well. Strain into chilled martini glasses. Garnish with a lemon twist.

Liar's Martini

6 parts Gin
2 parts Dry Vermouth
1 part Triple Sec
1 part Sweet Vermouth

Pour ingredients into a shaker with cracked ice and shake well.
Strain into chilled martini glasses. Garnish with an orange twist.

Limon Martini

2 parts Bacardi Limon Rum
1 part Dry Vermouth

Pour ingredients into a shaker with cracked ice and shake well.
Strain into chilled martini glasses. Garnish with a lemon twist.

Love Martini

2 parts Gin
1 part Green Curaçao

Pour ingredients into a shaker with cracked ice and shake well.
Strain into chilled martini glasses. Garnish with a lemon twist.

Low Tide Martini

6 parts Vodka
1 part Dry Vermouth
1 tsp Clam Juice

Place a smoked clam into chilled martini glasses. Pour ingredients
into a shaker with cracked ice and shake well. Strain into chilled
martini glasses. Garnish with a smoked clam stuffed olive and a
lemon twist.

Magnolia Blossom

4 parts Gin
1 part Lemon Juice
1 part Cream
1 drop Grenadine

Pour ingredients except Grenadine into a shaker with cracked ice
and shake well. Strain into chilled martini glasses. Add a drop of
Grenadine to each glass.

Magnum Opus Martini

8 parts Vodka
6 parts Crème de Cacao
1 part Peppermint Schnapps

Rim chilled martini glasses with shaved milk chocolate. In a shaker add 3 mint leaves, 1 strawberry and cracked ice. Shake to bruise and mix up leaves and strawberry. Add rest of the ingredients to shaker and shake vigorously. Strain into prepared martini glasses.

Mai Tai Martini

4 parts Vodka
1 part Dry Vermouth
1 part Orange Curaçao
1 part Pineapple Juice
1 part Orgeat Syrup

Pour ingredients into a shaker with cracked ice and shake well. Strain into chilled martini glasses. Garnish with a pineapple wheel and a cherry.

Maiden's Dream

6 parts Gin
3 parts Pernod
1 part Grenadine

Pour ingredients into a shaker with cracked ice and shake well. Strain into chilled martini glasses. Garnish with a lemon twist.

Mama's Martini

6 parts Vanilla Vodka
1 part Apricot Brandy
5 dashes Bitters
5 dashes Lemon Juice

Pour ingredients into a shaker with cracked ice and shake well. Strain into chilled martini glasses. Garnish with a lemon twist.

Manhasset

8 parts Rye Whiskey
1 part Dry Vermouth
1 part Sweet Vermouth
2 parts Lemon Juice

Pour ingredients into a shaker with cracked ice and shake well. Strain into chilled martini glasses. Garnish with a lemon twist.

Martini Quid Pro Quo

2 parts Vodka
1 part Extra Dry Vermouth
2 dashes Cherry Brandy
1 drop Vanilla Extract

Pour ingredients except Vanilla Extract into a shaker with cracked ice and shake well. Open shaker, add Vanilla Extract and swirl once. Strain into chilled martini glasses. Garnish with an olive.

Martini Quid Pro Quo 2

2 parts Vanilla Vodka
1 part Extra Dry Vermouth
1 part Cherry Brandy

Pour ingredients into a shaker with cracked ice and shake well. Strain into chilled martini glasses. Garnish with an olive.

Martini Stinger

2 parts Gin
1 part Crème de Menthe

Pour ingredients into a shaker with cracked ice and shake well. Strain into chilled martini glasses. Garnish with a mint sprig.

Martini Thyme

3 parts Gin
1 part Green Chartreuse

Pour ingredients into a shaker with cracked ice and shake well. Strain into chilled martini glasses. Garnish with a sprig of thyme.

Martini Without a Name

12 parts Vodka
2 parts Cointreau
1 part Green Chartreuse

Pour ingredients into a shaker with cracked ice and shake well. Strain into chilled martini glasses. Garnish with an orange twist.

Martinrena

6 parts Vodka
2 parts Tequila
1 part Dry Vermouth

Pour ingredients into a shaker with cracked ice and shake well. Strain into chilled martini glasses. Garnish with a lemon twist.

Metropolitan

12 parts Currant Vodka
2 parts Lillet Blanc
1 part Lime Juice

Pour ingredients into a shaker with cracked ice and shake well. Strain into chilled martini glasses. Garnish with a lime twist.

Metropolitan 2

6 parts Brandy
3 parts Sweet Vermouth
1 part Sugar Syrup
2 dashes Bitters

Pour ingredients into a shaker with cracked ice and shake well. Strain into chilled martini glasses. Garnish with a lemon twist.

Mets Manhattan

5 parts Whiskey
1 part Extra Dry Vermouth
1 part Strawberry Schnapps

Pour ingredients into a shaker with cracked ice and shake well. Strain into chilled martini glasses. Garnish with a fresh strawberry.

Mexiquita

1 part Tequila
1 part Melon Liqueur
1 splash Lime Juice
1 splash Soda Water

Pour all ingredients except soda water into a shaker with cracked ice and shake well. Strain into chilled martini glasses. Top each glass with soda water and garnish with a lime twist.

Midnight Black Martini

6 parts Vodka
1 part Black Sambuca

Pour ingredients into a shaker with cracked ice and shake well. Strain into chilled martini glasses. Garnish with fresh Bing cherries.

Midnight Martini

3 parts Vodka
1 part Raspberry Liqueur

Pour ingredients into a shaker with cracked ice and shake well. Strain into chilled martini glasses. Garnish with fresh raspberries.

Midnight Sun Martini

5 parts Cranberry Vodka
1 part Vodka
1 part Kahlua

Pour ingredients into a shaker with cracked ice and shake well. Strain into chilled martini glasses.

Millennium Martini

8 parts Vodka
2 parts Triple Sec
2 parts Banana Liqueur
1 part Raspberry Liqueur
3 parts Apple Juice

Pour ingredients into a shaker with cracked ice and shake well. Strain into chilled martini glasses. Garnish with raspberries.

Millennium Martini 2

6 parts Vodka
1 part Jägermeister
1 part Cranberry Juice

Pour ingredients into a shaker with cracked ice and shake well. Strain into chilled martini glasses. Garnish with a lime twist.

Mistico Martini

1 part Jose Cuervo Mistico
1 part Chambord
1 part Sour Mix

Pour ingredients into a shaker with cracked ice and shake well. Strain into chilled martini glasses. Garnish with a lime wedge.

Monkey Gland Martini

8 parts Gin
8 parts Orange Juice
1 part Anise
1 part Grenadine

Pour ingredients into a shaker with cracked ice and shake well. Strain into chilled martini glasses. Garnish with an orange twist.

Moon Dust Martini

4 parts Vodka
1 part Goldschläger

Rim chilled martini glasses with lime and dip into crushed peppermints to coat. Pour ingredients into a shaker with cracked ice and shake well. Strain into prepared glasses.

Muffy Martini

1 part Lemon Vodka
1 part Triple Sec
1 part Peach Schnapps
1 splash Orange Juice

Pour ingredients into a shaker with cracked ice and shake well. Strain into chilled martini glasses. Garnish with fresh Bing cherries.

Mystical Martini

4 parts Mezcal
1 part Lillet

Pour ingredients into a shaker with cracked ice and shake well. Strain into chilled martini glasses. Garnish with a lemon twist and an orange twist.

Naughty by Nature

4 parts Raspberry Vodka
1 part Triple Sec
1 part Cranberry Juice
1 splash Lime Juice

Pour ingredients into a shaker with cracked ice and shake well. Strain into chilled martini glasses. Garnish with fresh blackberries.

Newbury Martini

6 parts Gin
2 parts Sweet Vermouth
1 part Triple Sec

Pour ingredients into a shaker with cracked ice and shake well. Strain into chilled martini glasses. Garnish with a lemon twist.

Oakland Martini

2 parts Vodka
1 part Dry Vermouth
1 part Orange Juice

Pour ingredients into a shaker with cracked ice and shake well. Strain into chilled martini glasses. Garnish with an orange wedge.

Oh My God!

4 parts Vodka
2 parts Tequila
1 part Dark Rum
1 part 151 Proof Rum

Pour all ingredients except the 151 proof rum into a shaker with cracked ice and shake well. Strain into chilled martini glasses. Top with the 151 proof rum. Garnish with a lime twist. Light martini on fire.

Old Country Martini

3 parts Vodka
1 part Madeira Wine
1 part Cherry Brandy

Pour ingredients into a shaker with cracked ice and shake well. Strain into chilled martini glasses. Garnish with an orange twist.

Old Fashioned Martini

12 parts Vodka
1 part Bourbon
2 dashes Bitters
2 tsp Sugar
2 wedges of Orange, Lime & Lemon

Pour ingredients into a shaker with cracked ice and shake well. Strain into chilled martini glasses. Garnish with a cherry.

Opal Martini

6 parts Gin
1 part Triple Sec
2 parts Orange Juice
1/4 tsp Bar Sugar

Pour ingredients into a shaker with cracked ice and shake well. Strain into chilled martini glasses. Garnish with an orange wedge.

Opal Martini 2

2 parts Gin
2 parts Orange Juice
1 part Orange Liqueur

Pour ingredients into a shaker with cracked ice and shake well. Strain into chilled martini glasses.

Opera Martini

6 parts Gin
2 parts Dubonnet Blanc
1 part Maraschino Liqueur

Pour ingredients into a shaker with cracked ice and shake well. Strain into chilled martini glasses. Garnish with a lemon twist.

Opus

6 parts Vodka
1 part Beer
3 parts Dry Vermouth

Pour ingredients into a shaker with cracked ice and shake well. Strain into chilled martini glasses. Garnish with a cherry.

Original French Martini

1 part Orange Liqueur
1 part Raspberry Liqueur
1 part Sour Mix

Pour ingredients into a shaker with cracked ice and shake well. Strain into chilled martini glasses.

Pall Mall Martini

4 parts Gin
1 part Dry Vermouth
1 part Sweet Vermouth
1 tsp Crème de Menthe
1 dash Bitters

Pour ingredients into a shaker with cracked ice and shake well. Strain into chilled martini glasses. Garnish with an orange peel.

Parrothead Martini

6 parts Tequila
1 part Triple Sec
1 part Lime Juice

Pour ingredients into a shaker with cracked ice and shake well. Strain into chilled martini glasses. Garnish with a lime twist.

Passionate Ruby Kiss

2 parts Vodka
1 part Alize Red Passion Fruit

Pour ingredients into a shaker with cracked ice and shake well. Strain into chilled martini glasses. Garnish with a lemon twist.

Pepper Martini

2 parts Pepper Vodka
1 part Dry Vermouth

Pour ingredients into a shaker with cracked ice and shake well. Strain into chilled martini glasses. Garnish with a jalapeno and an olive.

Petit Zinc Martini

2 parts Vodka
1 part Triple Sec
1 part Sweet Vermouth
1 part Orange Juice

Pour ingredients into a shaker with cracked ice and shake well. Strain into chilled martini glasses. Garnish with an orange wedge.

Pompano Martini

5 parts Gin
1 part Dry Vermouth
2 parts Grapefruit Juice
1 dash Bitters

Pour ingredients into a shaker with cracked ice and shake well. Strain into chilled martini glasses. Garnish with an orange twist.

Purple Butterfly

3 parts Gin
1 part Cherry Brandy
1 splash Blue Curaçao

Pour Gin and Curaçao into a shaker with cracked ice and shake well. Strain into chilled martini glasses. Garnish with a lemon twist.

Purple Nirple Martini

8 parts Vodka
2 parts Blue Curaçao
2 parts Cranberry Juice
1 part Grenadine
Juice of 1/2 Lime

Pour ingredients into a shaker with cracked ice and shake well. Strain into chilled martini glasses. Garnish with a lime wedge.

Red Dog Martini

12 parts Vodka
4 parts Ruby Port
2 parts Lime Juice
1 part Grenadine

Pour ingredients into a shaker with cracked ice and shake well. Strain into chilled martini glasses. Garnish with a lime twist.

Red Hot Martini

2 parts Vodka
1 part Cinnamon Liqueur

Pour ingredients into a shaker with cracked ice and shake well. Strain into chilled martini glasses. Garnish with a few cinnamon candies.

Red Rum

2 parts Vodka
1 part Chambord
1 part Crème de Cassis

Pour ingredients into a shaker with cracked ice and shake well. Strain into chilled martini glasses. Garnish with a lemon twist.

Red Tonic Martini

4 parts Vodka
1 part Grenadine
1 part Lemon Juice

Pour ingredients into a shaker with cracked ice and shake well. Strain into chilled martini glasses. Garnish with a lemon twist.

Red Velvet Martini

4 parts Vodka
2 parts Cranberry Juice
1 part Chambord
1 squeeze of fresh Lime Juice

Pour ingredients into a shaker with cracked ice and shake well. Strain into chilled martini glasses. Garnish with raspberries.

Regale

1 part Vodka
1 part Cinnamon Liqueur

Pour ingredients into a shaker with cracked ice and shake well. Strain into chilled martini glasses. Garnish with a single rose petal.

Renaissance Martini

6 parts Gin
1 part Fino Sherry

Pour ingredients into a shaker with cracked ice and shake well. Strain into chilled martini glasses. Garnish with grated nutmeg.

Rendezvous Martini

6 parts Gin
2 parts Cherry Brandy
1 part Campari

Pour ingredients into a shaker with cracked ice and shake well. Strain into chilled martini glasses. Garnish with a cherry.

Resolution Martini 2

6 parts Gin
2 parts Apricot Brandy
1 part Lemon Juice

Pour ingredients into a shaker with cracked ice and shake well. Strain into chilled martini glasses. Garnish with a lemon twist.

Riviera Martini

2 parts Vodka
1 part Chambord

Pour ingredients into a shaker with cracked ice and shake well. Strain into chilled martini glasses. Garnish with frozen raspberries.

Rolls Royce Martini

3 parts Gin
1 part Dry Vermouth
1 part Sweet Vermouth
1/4 tsp Bénédictine

Pour ingredients into a shaker with cracked ice and shake well. Strain into chilled martini glasses. Garnish with a lemon twist.

Roost Martini

6 parts Vodka
1 part Orange Brandy
1 part Almond Liqueur

Pour ingredients into a shaker with cracked ice and shake well. Strain into chilled martini glasses. Garnish with a sugar dipped orange.

Royal Martini

2 parts Crown Royal
1 part Dry Vermouth

Pour ingredients into a shaker with cracked ice and shake well. Strain into chilled martini glasses. Garnish with a lemon twist.

Rum Martini

6 parts Light Rum
1 part Dry Vermouth
1 dash Bitters

Pour ingredients into a shaker with cracked ice and shake well. Strain into chilled martini glasses. Garnish with an almond stuffed olive.

Sakétini

5 parts Gin or Vodka
2 parts Saké

Pour ingredients into a shaker with cracked ice and shake well. Strain into chilled martini glasses. Garnish with a slice of cucumber.

Sakétini 2

6 parts Gin
1 part Saké

Pour ingredients into a shaker with cracked ice and shake well. Strain into chilled martini glasses. Garnish with a lemon twist and a piece of pickled ginger.

Salt & Pepper

4 parts Pepper Vodka
1 part Dry Vermouth

Rim chilled martini glasses with salt. Pour ingredients into a shaker with cracked ice and shake well. Strain into prepared martini glasses. Garnish with an onion.

Sangratini

4 parts Red Wine
1 part Brandy
1 part Triple Sec
1 dash Orange Juice

Pour ingredients into a shaker with cracked ice and shake well. Strain into chilled martini glasses. Garnish with an orange slice.

Satan's Whiskers Martini
4 parts Gin
4 parts Dry Vermouth
4 parts Sweet Vermouth
4 parts Orange Juice
2 parts Triple Sec
1 part Bitters

Pour ingredients into a shaker with cracked ice and shake well. Strain into chilled martini glasses. Garnish with an orange twist.

Scofflaw Martini
4 parts Vodka
4 parts Rye
4 parts Dry Vermouth
1 part Lemon Juice

Pour ingredients into a shaker with cracked ice and shake well. Strain into chilled martini glasses. Garnish with a dash of Grenadine and a lemon twist.

Screaming Orgasm
2 parts Vodka
1 part Amaretto Liqueur
1 part Kahlua
1 part Cream

Pour ingredients into a shaker with cracked ice and shake well. Strain into chilled martini glasses. Garnish with shaved chocolate.

Sex at Sunset
4 parts Vodka
3 parts Sweet Red Vermouth
2 parts Frangelico Hazelnut Liqueur
2 parts Amaretto

Pour ingredients into a shaker with cracked ice and shake well. Strain into chilled martini glasses.

Sex with an Alligator
2 parts Coconut Rum
2 parts Midori Melon Liqueur
2 parts Pineapple Juice
1 part Jägermeister
1 splash Chambord

Pour Rum, Midori and Pineapple Juice into a shaker with cracked ice and shake well. Strain into chilled martini glasses. Drizzle in Chambord and let settle on bottom of glass. Top with Jägermeister.

Sexy Devil

4 parts Vodka
2 parts Cranberry Vodka
1 part Dry Vermouth

Pour ingredients into a shaker with cracked ice and shake well. Strain into chilled martini glasses. Garnish with a lemon peel and a strawberry.

Shrimptini

3 parts Gin or Vodka
1 part Dry Vermouth
1 dash Tabasco

Pour ingredients into a shaker with cracked ice and shake well. Strain into chilled martini glasses. Garnish with large cooked shrimp.

Sidecar Martini

3 parts Vodka
3 parts Brandy
2 parts Lemon Juice
3 parts Cointreau

Rim chilled martini glasses with sugar. Pour ingredients into a shaker with cracked ice and shake well. Strain into prepared martini glasses. Garnish with a lime twist.

Silver Streak

2 parts Gin or Vodka
1 part Jägermeister

Pour ingredients into a shaker with cracked ice and shake well. Strain into chilled martini glasses. Garnish with a lemon twist.

Single Malt Martini

3 parts Single Malt Scotch
1 part Fino Sherry

Pour ingredients into a shaker with cracked ice and shake well. Strain into chilled martini glasses. Garnish with a lemon peel.

Sling Martini

2 parts Gin
1 part Cherry Brandy
1 part Lemon Juice

Pour ingredients into a shaker with cracked ice and shake well. Strain into chilled martini glasses. Garnish with a lemon twist.

Slo Comfortable Screw Martini

4 parts Vodka
4 parts Southern Comfort
2 parts Gin
1 part Galliano

Pour all ingredients except Galliano into a shaker with cracked ice and shake well. Strain into chilled martini glasses. Top glasses with Galliano.

Smoke on the Water

8 parts Vodka
1 part Raspberry Liqueur

Pour ingredients into a shaker with cracked ice and shake well. Strain into chilled martini glasses. Garnish with an orange wedge.

Smoked Salmon Martini

8 parts Vodka
1 part Dry Vermouth

Pour ingredients into a shaker with cracked ice and shake well. Strain into chilled martini glasses. Garnish with smoked salmon stuffed olive, egg, onion & capers.

Snake Bite Martini

6 parts Vodka
1 part Triple Sec
1 part Tequila
Juice of one fresh orange

Pour ingredients into a shaker with cracked ice and shake well. Strain into chilled martini glasses. Garnish with an orange wedge.

South of the Border

4 parts Vodka
1 part Triple Sec
1 part Sour Mix

Rim chilled martini glasses with salt. Pour ingredients into a shaker with cracked ice and shake well. Strain into prepared martini glasses. Garnish with a lemon twist.

Southern Martini

6 parts Gin
1 part Triple Sec
5 dashes Bitters

Pour ingredients into a shaker with cracked ice and shake well. Strain into chilled martini glasses. Garnish with a lemon twist.

Spanish Fly Martini

4 parts Spiced Rum
2 parts Dry Vermouth
1 part Southern Comfort
1 part Coffee Liqueur

Pour ingredients into a shaker with cracked ice and shake well. Strain into chilled martini glasses. Garnish with a pineapple wedge.

Spider Bite Martini

8 parts Infused Vodka
4 parts Coconut Rum
1 part Over Proof Rum
Few drops of Bitters

To infuse vodka: Combine 26 oz of Vodka with 1 part banana and 2 parts fresh (or canned) pineapple. Pour ingredients into a shaker with cracked ice and shake well. Strain into chilled martini glasses. Garnish with an orange twist and a cherry.

Springtime Martini

3 parts Buffalo Grass Vodka
1 part Lillet Blanc

Pour ingredients into a shaker with cracked ice and shake well. Strain into chilled martini glasses. Garnish with a pickled asparagus spear.

Starlight Martini

12 parts Vodka
4 parts Black Sambuca
1 part Dry Vermouth

Pour ingredients into a shaker with cracked ice and shake well. Strain into chilled martini glasses. Garnish with a lemon twist.

Staten Island Martini

6 parts Coffee Vodka
1 part Dry Vermouth
2 parts Lime Juice

Pour ingredients into a shaker with cracked ice and shake well. Strain into chilled martini glasses. Garnish with a chocolate covered cherry.

Stinger Martini

1 part Vodka
2 parts Brandy
1 part Crème de Menthe

Pour ingredients into a shaker with cracked ice and shake well. Strain into chilled martini glasses. Garnish with a fresh mint sprig.

Summertime Martini

2 parts Vodka
1 part Dry Vermouth
1 part Orange Juice

Pour ingredients into a shaker with cracked ice and shake well. Strain into chilled martini glasses. Garnish with an orange twist.

Super Model Martini

8 parts Bacardi Limon Rum
2 parts Melon Liqueur
2 parts Blue Curaçao Liqueur
1 part Dry Vermouth

Pour ingredients into a shaker with cracked ice and shake well. Strain into chilled martini glasses. Garnish with a lemon twist.

Swinger Martini

6 parts Vodka
3 parts Gin
2 parts Lime Cordial

Rim chilled martini glasses with Dry Vermouth. Pour ingredients into a shaker with cracked ice and shake well. Strain into chilled martini glasses. Garnish with a lemon twist.

Take Five Martini

2 parts Vodka
1 part Green Curaçao Liqueur
1 part Lime Juice

Pour ingredients into a shaker with cracked ice and shake well. Strain into chilled martini glasses. Garnish with a lime wedge.

Tequila Fanny Banger Martini

8 parts Vodka
8 parts Tequila
8 parts Midori Melon Liqueur
1 part Triple Sec
1 part Lime Juice

Pour ingredients into a shaker with cracked ice and shake well. Strain into chilled martini glasses. Garnish with a lime twist.

Tequila Sunset

1 part White Tequila
1 part White Rum
1 splash Grenadine
1 part Orange Juice

Pour tequila and rum into a shaker with cracked ice and shake well. Strain into chilled martini glasses. Fill with orange juice and float the Grenadine. Garnish with an orange slice.

Tequini

2 parts Tequila
1 part Dry Vermouth

Pour ingredients into a shaker with cracked ice and shake well. Strain into chilled martini glasses. Garnish with a lime twist and an olive.

Tequini 2

6 parts Tequila
1 part Dry Vermouth
1 dash Bitters

Pour ingredients into a shaker with cracked ice and shake well. Strain into chilled martini glasses. Garnish with a lime twist.

The Glass Cleaner

1 part Gin
1 part Blue Curaçao Liqueur
3 parts White Grape Juice

Pour ingredients into a shaker with cracked ice and shake well. Strain into chilled martini glasses.

The Marvelous Martini

3 parts Vodka
1 part Sweet Vermouth
1 part Cranberry Juice

Pour ingredients into a shaker with cracked ice and shake well. Strain into chilled martini glasses. Garnish with a cocktail onion.

The Viagra Martini

1 part Vodka
1 part Lemon Vodka
1 part Orange Vodka
1 part Orange Liqueur
1 part Cranberry Juice
1 splash Lime Juice

Pour ingredients into a shaker with cracked ice and shake well. Strain into chilled martini glasses. Garnish with a lemon twist. When mixed this drink is the colour of Viagra.

Tie Me to the Bedposts

1 part Citrus Vodka
1 part Midori Melon Liqueur
1 part Coconut Rum
1 splash Sour Mix

Pour ingredients into a shaker with cracked ice and shake well. Strain into chilled martini glasses.

Tom Collintini

2 parts Gin
1 part Lemon Juice
1 tsp Sugar

Pour ingredients into a shaker with cracked ice and shake well. Strain into chilled martini glasses. Garnish with a lemon twist.

Tovarisch Martini

3 parts Vodka
1 part Kummel
1 part Lime Juice

Pour ingredients into a shaker with cracked ice and shake well. Strain into chilled martini glasses. Garnish with a black olive.

Turf Martini

4 parts Gin
2 parts Dry Vermouth
1 part Pernod
1 part Lemon Juice
5 dashes Bitters

Pour ingredients into a shaker with cracked ice and shake well. Strain into chilled martini glasses. Garnish with an almond stuffed olive.

Tuxedo Martini

4 parts Vodka
3 parts Dry Vermouth
1 part Maraschino Liqueur
5 dashes Bitters

Pour ingredients into a shaker with cracked ice and shake well. Strain into chilled martini glasses. Garnish with a lemon twist.

Two Blue Martini

4 parts Vodka
4 parts Gin
1 part Cognac

Pour ingredients into a shaker with cracked ice and shake well. Strain into chilled martini glasses. Garnish with two blue cheese stuffed olives.

Ulanda Martini

4 parts Gin
2 parts Triple Sec
1 part Pernod

Pour ingredients into a shaker with cracked ice and shake well. Strain into chilled martini glasses. Garnish with an orange twist.

Under the Volcano Martini

4 parts Mezcal
1 part Dry Vermouth

Pour ingredients into a shaker with cracked ice and shake well. Strain into chilled martini glasses. Garnish with a jalapeno stuffed olive.

Vampire Proof Martini

4 parts Gin or Vodka
1 part Dry Vermouth

Pour ingredients into a shaker with cracked ice and shake well. Strain into chilled martini glasses. Garnish with a garlic stuffed olive.

Vanilla Twist Martini

6 parts Vanilla Vodka
1 part Cointreau
1 part Dry Vermouth

Pour ingredients into a shaker with cracked ice and shake well. Strain into chilled martini glasses. Garnish with a vanilla bean.

Veggie Martini

4 parts Gin or Vodka
1 part Dry Vermouth

Pour ingredients into a shaker with cracked ice and shake well. Strain into chilled martini glasses. Garnish with a green olive, a black olive, an onion and a baby carrot.

Vegetini

5 parts Vodka
1 part Sweet Vermouth

Pour ingredients into a shaker with cracked ice and shake well. Strain into chilled martini glasses. Garnish with a sun dried tomato stuffed olive.

Velour

3 parts Vodka
1 part Cranberry Juice
1 part Blue Curaçao

Pour ingredients into a shaker with cracked ice and shake well. Strain into chilled martini glasses.

Very Black Martini

4 parts Black Vodka
1 part Raspberry Liqueur
1 splash Cranberry Juice

Pour ingredients into a shaker with cracked ice and shake well. Strain into chilled martini glasses. Garnish with a lemon twist.

Volga Volga Martini

2 parts Vodka
1 part Blue Curaçao Liqueur
1 drop Pernod

Pour ingredients into a shaker with cracked ice and shake well. Strain into chilled martini glasses. Garnish with a lemon twist.

Ward 8 Martini

4 parts Vodka
4 parts Bourbon
2 parts Orange Juice
2 parts Lemon Juice
1 part Grenadine

Pour all ingredients except Grenadine into a shaker with cracked ice and shake well. Strain into chilled martini glasses. Top with a dash of Grenadine. Garnish with an orange slice.

Warm Blonde

1 part Southern Comfort
1 part Amaretto

Pour ingredients into a shaker with cracked ice and shake well. Strain into chilled martini glasses. Garnish with several thin lemon rind spirals.

Wave Martini

1 part Vodka
1 part Gin
1 part Midori Melon Liqueur
1 part Triple Sec

Pour ingredients into a shaker with cracked ice and shake well. Strain into chilled martini glasses. Garnish with a lemon twist.

White, White Russian Martini

1 part Vodka
1 part White Chocolate Liqueur
1 part Kahlua

Pour ingredients into a shaker with cracked ice and shake well. Strain into chilled martini glasses. Garnish with a cherry.

Xiantha

1 part Gin
1 part Cherry Brandy
1 part Yellow Chartreuse

Pour ingredients into a shaker with cracked ice and shake well. Strain into chilled martini glasses. Garnish with a cherry.

Yellow Rose Martini

3 parts Spiced Rum
1 part Sweet Red Vermouth
1 splash Ouzo

Pour a splash of Ouzo into chilled martini glasses and swirl to coat. Pour remaining ingredients into a shaker with cracked ice and shake well. Strain into prepared martini glasses. Garnish with a cherry.

Yellow Snowman

2 parts Lemon Vodka
2 parts Lemon Rum
2 parts Peppermint Schnapps
1 part Bailey's
6 mint leaves

Pour all ingredients except Bailey's into a shaker with cracked ice and shake well. Place an ice cube into each chilled martini glass. Pour shaken mixture into prepared glasses. Drip Bailey's on top for a 'snowy' effect.

You're Fired Martini

8 parts Vodka
4 parts Bailey's
2 parts Amber Rum
1 part Coffee Liqueur
1 part Crème de Cacao
1 part Milk

Rim chilled martini glasses with sugar. Pour ingredients into a shaker with cracked ice and shake well. Strain into chilled martini glasses.

Zippy Martini

6 parts Vodka
1 part Dry Vermouth
4 dashes Tabasco

Pour ingredients into a shaker with cracked ice and shake well. Strain into chilled martini glasses. Garnish with a pickled jalapeno.

THE CONFECTIONS

A Drink with Something In It

There is something about a Martini,
A tingle remarkably pleasant,
A yellow, a mellow Martini,
I wish I had one present.

There is something about a Martini,
Ere the dining and dancing begin,
And to tell you the truth,
It's not the vermouth —
I think that perhaps it's the gin.

— Ogden Nash —

After Eight Martini

2 parts Vodka
2 parts White Crème de Cacao
1 part White Crème de Menthe

Pour ingredients into a shaker with cracked ice and shake well. Strain into chilled martini glasses. Garnish with a cherry.

After Eight Martini 2

1 part Vodka
2 parts Bailey's
1 part Green Crème de Menthe

Pour ingredients into a shaker with cracked ice and shake well. Strain into chilled martini glasses. Garnish with a cherry.

All-Star Martini

8 parts Vodka
2 parts White Chocolate Liqueur
1 part Scotch

Pour ingredients into a shaker with cracked ice and shake well. Strain into chilled martini glasses. Garnish with shaved chocolate.

Almond Joy Martini

16 parts Vodka
1 part Hazelnut Liqueur
1 part Crème de Cacao
1 dash Coconut syrup

Pour ingredients into a shaker with cracked ice and shake well. Strain into chilled martini glasses. Garnish with 1 roasted, unsalted almond.

Alternatini

8 parts Vodka
1 part Sweet Vermouth
1 part Dry Vermouth
2 parts White Crème de Cacao

Rim chilled martini glasses with sweetened coco powder. Pour ingredients into a shaker with cracked ice and shake well. Strain into chilled martini glasses. Garnish with a Hershey Kiss.

Amy's Chocolate Jack

2 parts Vodka
2 parts Dry Vermouth
2 parts White Crème de Cacao
1 part Jack Daniels Bourbon

Pour ingredients into a shaker with cracked ice and shake well. Strain into chilled martini glasses. Garnish with shaved dark chocolate. *Hint: If you prefer a sweeter drink add more Crème de Cacao.*

Apple Pie Martini

6 parts Vanilla Vodka
1 part Calvados
1 part Dry Vermouth

Pour ingredients into a shaker with cracked ice and shake well. Strain into chilled martini glasses. Garnish with an apple slice.

Banana Split Martini

6 parts Vodka
3 parts Crème de Cacao
1 part Banana Liqueur
Few drops of Grenadine

Pour ingredients, except Grenadine, into a shaker with cracked ice and shake well. Strain into chilled martini glasses. Add a few drops of Grenadine to glasses and top with whipped cream and banana slice. *Hint: to keep banana slices from browning, toss with fresh lemon juice and keep chilled.*

Bon Bon Martini

3 parts Vodka
2 parts White Crème de Cacao
1 splash Triple Sec

Pour ingredients into a shaker with cracked ice and shake twice only. Strain into chilled martini glasses. Garnish with shaved white chocolate.

Bourbon Bon Bon

2 parts Vodka
2 parts Dry Vermouth
2 parts White Crème de Cacao
1 part Bourbon

Pour ingredients into a shaker with cracked ice and shake well. Strain into chilled martini glasses. Garnish with shaved chocolate.

Brandy Alexander

1 part Brandy
1 part Dark Crème de Cacao
1 part Cream

Pour ingredients into a shaker with cracked ice and shake well. Strain into chilled martini glasses. Sprinkle with cinnamon and nutmeg.

Brassass Brunch

3 parts Vodka
1 part Hazelnut Liqueur
2 parts Hot Coffee

Pour ingredients into a heat resistant container stir gently. Pour into heat resistant glasses and top with whipped cream and a roasted hazelnut.

BS Martini

9 parts Vanilla Vodka
4 parts Kahlua
1 splash Chocolate Syrup

Pour ingredients into a shaker with cracked ice and shake well. Strain into chilled martini glasses. Garnish with a Hershey's Kiss.

Buff Martini

5 parts Vodka
1 part Kahlua
1 part Irish Cream

Add all ingredients over ice, stir gently and strain into chilled martini glasses. Add a sprinkle of freshly ground coffee or cinnamon.

Butterscotch Martini

2 parts Vodka
1 part Butterscotch Schnapps

Pour ingredients into a shaker with cracked ice and shake well. Strain into chilled martini glasses. Garnish with butterscotch chips.

Butterscotch Sundae

2 parts Vodka
1 part Crème de Cacao
1 part Butterscotch Schnapps

Pour ingredients into a shaker with cracked ice and shake well. Strain into chilled martini glasses. Garnish with whipped cream and a cherry.

Buzz Ball Martini

16 parts Coffee Vodka
1 part Kahlua
1 part White Crème de Cacao

Pour ingredients into a shaker with cracked ice and shake well. Strain into chilled martini glasses. Garnish with a chocolate covered coffee bean.

Candini

12 parts Vodka
1 part Apricot Brandy
1 part Orange Brandy
1 part Sweet Vermouth
1 part Lime Cordial

Pour ingredients into a shaker with cracked ice and shake well. Strain into chilled martini glasses. Garnish with an orange wedge.

Candy Apple Martini

1 part Zinamon Vodka
1 part Sour Apple Schnapps
2 parts Apple Juice
1 splash Amaretto

Prepare glasses ahead by dipping rims in red candy apple coating and chill in freezer. Just prior to mixing pour a splash of Amaretto into each glass and swirl. Pour remaining ingredients into a shaker with cracked ice and shake well. Strain into prepared glasses. Garnish with an apple slice.

Caramel Martini

1 part Butter Ripple Schnapps
1 part Vodka

Pour ingredients into a shaker with cracked ice and shake well. Strain into chilled martini glasses.

Caramilk

3 parts Vodka
2 parts White Crème de Cacao
1 part Caramel Flavouring

Pour ingredients into a shaker with cracked ice and shake well. Strain into chilled martini glasses. Garnish with shaved milk chocolate.

Chetta O Chocola

3 parts Vodka
2 parts Chambord
1 part Godiva Chocolate Liqueur
1 splash Pineapple Juice

Pour ingredients into a shaker with cracked ice and shake well. Strain into chilled martini glasses. Garnish with pineapple pieces.

Chick's Chocolate Martini

3 parts Vodka
1 part Sweet Vermouth
1 splash Chocolate Syrup

Pour ingredients into a shaker with cracked ice and shake well. Strain into chilled martini glasses. Garnish with shaved chocolate.

Choco-Coconutini

1 part Vodka
1 part Crème de Cacao
1 part Coconut Rum

Pour ingredients into a shaker with cracked ice and shake well. Strain into chilled martini glasses. Garnish with shaved chocolate.

Chocolate Cherry Martini

2 parts Vodka
2 parts Crème de Cacao
1 part Cherry Brandy

Pour ingredients into a shaker with cracked ice and shake well. Strain into chilled martini glasses. Garnish with a cherry.

Chocolate Cherry Martini 2

2 parts Vodka
2 parts Cherry Brandy
1 part White Crème de Cacao

Rim martini glasses with melted chocolate and place in freezer to harden the chocolate. Pour ingredients into a shaker with cracked ice and shake well. Strain into prepared martini glasses. Garnish with a chocolate dipped cherry.

Chocolate Covered Strawberry

2 parts Strawberry Vodka
1 part White Crème de Cacao

Pour ingredients into a shaker with cracked ice and shake well. Strain into chilled martini glasses. Garnish with a fresh strawberry dipped in chocolate.

Chocolate Covered Strawberry 2

1 part Strawberry Vodka
1 part Godiva White Chocolate Liqueur

Pour ingredients into a shaker with cracked ice and shake well. Strain into chilled martini glasses. Garnish with chocolate chips.

Chocolate Devil Martini

3 parts Vodka
1 part Crème de Cacao
1 part Melon Liqueur
1 part Cranberry Juice
1 part Orange Juice

Pour ingredients into a shaker with cracked ice and shake well. Strain into chilled martini glasses. Garnish with an orange wedge.

Chocolate Dreams

2 parts Vodka
1 part Bailey's
1 part Crème de Cacao

Pour ingredients into a shaker with cracked ice and shake well. Strain into chilled martini glasses. Top glasses with whipped cream and a drizzle of Bailey's.

Chocolate Lemon

1 part Vodka
1 part Crème de Cacao
1 part Lemon Liqueur

Pour ingredients into a shaker with cracked ice and shake well. Strain into chilled martini glasses. Garnish with a chocolate dipped lemon slice.

Chocolate Martini

6 parts Vodka
1 part Crème de Cacao

Pour ingredients into a shaker with cracked ice and shake well. Strain into chilled martini glasses. Garnish with a single chocolate curl.

Chocolate Martini 2

2 parts Vodka
1 part Godiva White Chocolate Liqueur

Pour ingredients into a shaker with cracked ice and shake well. Strain into chilled martini glasses. Garnish with a lemon twist.

Chocolate Monkey

6 parts Vodka
5 parts Crème de Cacao
1 part Banana Liqueur

Pour ingredients into a shaker with cracked ice and shake well. Strain into chilled martini glasses. Garnish with chocolate dipped banana slice.

Chocolate Orange

2 parts Vodka
2 parts Crème de Cacao
1 part Orange Brandy

Pour ingredients into a shaker with cracked ice and shake well. Strain into chilled martini glasses. Garnish with an orange wedge.

Chocolatta Sweetie

1 part Vodka
1 part Amaretto
1 part Kahlua
1 part Bailey's

Pour all ingredients except Bailey's into a shaker with cracked ice and shake well. Strain into chilled martini glasses. Top glasses with Bailey's.

Chocotini

1 part Vodka
1 part Crème de Cacao

Pour ingredients into a shaker with cracked ice and shake well. Strain into chilled martini glasses. Garnish with an orange twist.

Christmas Bonus Martini

16 parts Vodka
1 part Peppermint Schnapps

Rim chilled glasses with lemon and coat with crushed candy cane. Pour ingredients into a shaker with cracked ice and shake well. Strain into chilled martini glasses. Garnish with a mini candy cane.

Christmas Martini

6 parts Vodka
1 part Peppermint Schnapps
1 splash Cranberry Juice

Rim chilled martini glasses with "Fairy Dust" mix. Pour ingredients into a shaker with cracked ice and shake well for 10 - 15 seconds. Strain into chilled martini glasses. Garnish with a mini candy cane. *Fairy Dust: 3 parts powdered sugar and 1 part very finely crushed candy canes.*

Christmas Martini 2

12 parts Vodka
2 parts Dry Vermouth
1 part Peppermint Schnapps

Pour ingredients into a shaker with cracked ice and shake well. Strain into chilled martini glasses. Garnish with a mini candy cane.

Christminti

1 part Vanilla Vodka
1 part White Crème de Cacao
1 part Green Crème de Menthe

Pour ingredients into a shaker with cracked ice and shake well. Strain into chilled martini glasses. Garnish with shaved chocolate.

Cocoa Peach Martini

2 parts Vodka
1 part Coconut Rum
1 part Peach Schnapps
2 parts Cranberry Juice

Pour ingredients into a shaker with cracked ice and shake well. Strain into chilled martini glasses. Garnish with a peach wedge and sprinkle with coconut.

Coconut Chocolate Sundae

4 parts Infused Vodka
1 part White Chocolate Liqueur
1 part Dark Crème de Cacao

Infuse vodka with the meat of one coconut. Pour ingredients into a shaker with cracked ice and shake well. Strain into chilled martini glasses. Garnish with a cherry and a drizzle of chocolate syrup.

Coffee Lover's Martini

6 parts Coffee Vodka
1 part Dry Vermouth
1 part Frangelico Hazelnut Liqueur

Pour ingredients into a shaker with cracked ice and shake well. Strain into chilled martini glasses. Garnish with a coffee bean.

Coffee Martini

4 parts Vanilla Vodka
2 parts Coffee Liqueur
1 part chilled Espresso

Pour ingredients into a shaker with cracked ice and shake very well. Strain into chilled martini glasses. Garnish with a chocolate covered coffee bean.

Dazed and Infused

12 parts Infused Vodka
1 part Bailey's

To infuse vodka: Combine 26oz vodka with roasted vanilla beans, macadamia nuts and cinnamon. Pour ingredients into a shaker with cracked ice and shake well. Strain into chilled martini glasses. Garnish with caramelized sugar.

Decadent Martini

6 parts Vodka
2 parts Amaretto
1 part Raspberry Liqueur

Pour ingredients into a shaker with cracked ice and shake well. Strain into chilled martini glasses. Garnish with a Hershey's Kiss.

Decadent Martini 2

12 parts Vodka
2 parts Raspberry Liqueur
1 part Amaretto

Pour ingredients into a shaker with cracked ice and shake well. Strain into chilled martini glasses. Garnish with a Hershey's Kiss.

Delicious Martini

6 parts Coffee Vodka
1 part Triple Sec

Pour ingredients into a shaker with cracked ice and shake well. Strain into chilled martini glasses. Garnish with an orange twist.

Double Fudge Martini

6 parts Vodka
1 part Coffee Liqueur
1 part Chocolate Liqueur

Pour ingredients into a shaker with cracked ice and shake well. Strain into chilled martini glasses. Garnish with a chocolate cocktail straw.

Double Fudge Swirl Martini

1 part Chocolate Vodka
1 part White Chocolate Liqueur
1 part Vanilla Vodka
1 splash Licor 43

Pour all ingredients except Licor 43 into a shaker with cracked ice and shake well. Strain into chilled martini glasses. Add Licor 43 to top of martinis slowly in a swirling motion.

Double S&M Martini

16 parts Vodka
2 parts Sambuca
1 part Green Crème de Menthe

Pour ingredients into a shaker with cracked ice and shake well. Strain into chilled martini glasses. Garnish with a scotch mint.

Dreamsicle Martini

1 part Vanilla Vodka
1 splash Dry Vermouth
1 splash Sweet Vermouth
1 splash Orange Juice

Pour ingredients into a shaker with cracked ice and shake well. Strain into chilled martini glasses. Garnish with an orange twist.

Fantasitini

2 parts Vanilla Vodka
1 part White Crème de Cacao
1 part Jägermeister

Pour all ingredients except Jägermeister into a shaker with cracked ice and shake well. Pour Jägermeister into the bottom of chilled martini glasses. Slowly pour shaken ingredients on top of Jägermeister for a layer effect.

Festive Martini

6 parts Egg Nog
2 parts Vodka
1 part Irish Cream
1 part White Chocolate Liqueur

Pour ingredients into a shaker with cracked ice and shake well. Strain into chilled martini glasses. Garnish with a cherry and sprinkle with cinnamon.

Golden Nugget Martini

8 parts Vodka
1 part Hazelnut Liqueur

Pour ingredients into a shaker with cracked ice and shake well. Strain into chilled martini glasses. Garnish with roasted pine nuts.

Grape Freshitini

1 part Currant Vodka
1 splash Raspberry Liqueur
1 splash Lime Juice

Rim glasses with sugar. Pour ingredients into a shaker with cracked ice and shake well. Strain into chilled martini glasses. Garnish with green grapes.

Gumdrop Martini

8 parts Lemon Rum
4 parts Vodka
2 parts Southern Comfort
1 part Dry Vermouth
2 parts Lemon Juice

Rim glasses with sugar. Pour ingredients into a shaker with cracked ice and shake well. Strain into chilled martini glasses. Garnish with a lemon slice and gumdrops.

Halloween Martini

2 parts Vodka
1 part TGIF's Orange Dream

Pour ingredients into a shaker with cracked ice and shake well. Strain into chilled martini glasses. Garnish with an orange flavoured hard candy.

HopScotch Martini

2 parts Scotch
2 parts Butterscotch Schnapps
1 splash Sweet Vermouth

Pour ingredients into a shaker with cracked ice and shake well. Strain into chilled martini glasses. Garnish with two cherries.

Hot Sex

4 parts Vodka
2 parts Hot Chocolate
1 part Irish Cream
1 part Milk

Pour all ingredients except Hot Chocolate into a shaker with cracked ice and shake very well. Strain into chilled martini glasses. Top with Hot Chocolate and whipped cream. Garnish with shaved chocolate.

Iceberg Martini

2 parts Gin
2 parts Currant Vodka
1 part Lemon Vodka
1 splash Crème de Menthe

Pour ingredients into a shaker with cracked ice and shake well. Strain into chilled martini glasses. Garnish with a fresh sprig of mint.

Java Martini

3 parts Vodka
1 part Coffee Liqueur
1 part Dark Crème de Cacao
1 part Expresso

Pour ingredients into a shaker with cracked ice and shake well. Strain into chilled martini glasses. Garnish with chocolate covered coffee bean.

Key Lime Pie

3 parts Vodka
1 part Lime Juice
1 part Melon Liqueur
1 part Sweet Cream
1 dash of Bitters.

Rim glasses with graham cracker crumbs and chill. Pour ingredients into a shaker with cracked ice and shake well. Strain into prepared martini glasses.

Kroy-tini

2 parts Vodka
2 parts Chocolate Liqueur
1 part White Crème de Cacao
1 part Irish Cream
1 part Raspberry Liqueur

Rim martini glasses with melted chocolate and put in freezer to harden chocolate. Pour Vodka and Crème de Cacao into a shaker with cracked ice and shake well. Strain into prepared martini glasses. Pour Chocolate Liqueur, Irish Cream and Raspberry Liqueur into another shaker with cracked ice and shake well. Slowly strain to create at layer over first mixture. Garnish with chocolate shavings and raspberries.

Lemon Chiffon Martini

4 parts Vodka
1 part Triple Sec
1 squeeze of Lemon Juice

Pour ingredients into a shaker with cracked ice and shake well. Strain into chilled martini glasses. Garnish with a lemon twist.

Little Pink Lady

2 parts Vodka
1 part White Crème de Cacao
1 part White Chocolate Liqueur
1 splash Grenadine Syrup

Pour ingredients into a shaker with cracked ice and shake well. Strain into chilled martini glasses.

Macaroon Martini

6 parts Vodka
1 part Chocolate Liqueur
1 part Amaretto

Pour ingredients into a shaker with cracked ice and shake well. Strain into chilled martini glasses. Garnish with an orange twist.

Mint Martini

1 part Vodka
1 part Godiva White Chocolate Liqueur
1 splash Crème de Menthe

Pour ingredients into a shaker with cracked ice and shake well. Strain into chilled martini glasses. Garnish with a mint leaf.

Mocha Blanca Martini

3 parts Coffee Vodka
1 part White Chocolate Liqueur

Pour ingredients into a shaker with cracked ice and shake well. Strain into chilled martini glasses. Garnish with a single white chocolate curl.

Mocha Martini

4 parts Vanilla Vodka
1 part Cherry Liqueur
1 part Coffee Liqueur
1 part Irish Cream

Pour ingredients into a shaker with cracked ice and shake well. Strain into chilled martini glasses. Garnish with a cinnamon stick.

Mochatini

2 parts Gin
1 part Chocolate Liqueur
1 part Expresso

Pour ingredients into a shaker with cracked ice and shake well. Strain into chilled martini glasses. Garnish with two floating expresso beans.

Ninotchka Martini

6 parts Vanilla Vodka
2 parts White Chocolate Liqueur
1 part Lemon Juice

Pour ingredients into a shaker with cracked ice and shake well. Strain into chilled martini glasses. Garnish with a lemon twist.

No. 1 Cafe Cerise

2 parts Vodka
1 part Raspberry Liqueur
1 part Coffee Liqueur

Pour ingredients into a shaker with cracked ice and shake well. Strain into chilled martini glasses. Garnish with a cherry and chocolate shavings.

Nutty Butty

2 parts Vodka
1 part Southern Comfort
1 part Amaretto

Pour ingredients into a shaker with cracked ice and shake well.
Strain into chilled martini glasses.

Nutty Martini

1 part Vodka or Gin
1 part Amaretto

Pour ingredients into a shaker with cracked ice and shake well.
Strain into chilled martini glasses. Garnish with an orange twist.

Nutty Martini 2

6 parts Vodka
1 part Frangelico Hazelnut Liqueur

Pour ingredients into a shaker with cracked ice and shake well.
Strain into chilled martini glasses.

Nutty Morgan

2 parts Spiced Rum
1 part Hazelnut Liqueur

Pour ingredients into a shaker with cracked ice and shake well.
Strain into chilled martini glasses.

Orange Cicle

4 parts Vanilla Vodka
1 part Triple Sec
1 splash Orange Juice

Pour ingredients into a shaker with cracked ice and shake well.
Strain into chilled martini glasses. Garnish with an orange twist.

Orange Icicle

1 part Orange Vodka
1 part Licor 43
1 part Cream

Pour ingredients into a shaker with cracked ice and shake well.
Strain into chilled martini glasses.

Orgasm Martini

2 parts Vodka
1 splash Triple Sec
1 splash White Crème de Cacao

Pour ingredients into a shaker with cracked ice and shake well. Strain into chilled martini glasses. Garnish with an orange twist.

Orgasmatini

3 parts Vodka
2 parts Crème de Cacao
1 part Bailey's

Pour ingredients into a shaker with cracked ice and shake well. Strain into chilled martini glasses. Garnish with a chocolate coated coffee bean.

Paradisio Martini

6 parts Infused Vodka
2 parts Amaretto
1 part Lime Cordial

To infuse vodka: Combine 26oz of vodka with 2 sliced pears, 1 orange, zest of half a lemon and 1/2 oz Poire William. Pour ingredients into a shaker with cracked ice and shake well. Strain into chilled martini glasses. Garnish with a pear slice and a lemon wedge.

Peanut Butter & Jelly Martini

2 parts Frangelico Hazelnut Liqueur
3 parts Raspberry Juice
3 parts Cranberry Vodka

Pour ingredients into a shaker with cracked ice and shake well. Strain into chilled martini glasses. Garnish with 2 raspberries. *Hint: You can make a raspberry slush instead and substitute for the juice.*

Peppermint Bon-Bomb

3 parts Vanilla Vodka
1 part Dark Crème de Cacao
2 dashes Crème de Menthe

Pour a puddle of chocolate syrup on a glass plate and chill. Rim chilled martini glasses with syrup. Pour ingredients into a shaker with cracked ice and shake well. Strain into prepared martini glasses.

Peppermint Martini

3 parts Vodka
1 part White Crème de Menthe

Pour ingredients into a shaker with cracked ice and shake well. Strain into chilled martini glasses. Garnish with a mint sprig.

Pudding Pop Martini

1 part Vodka
1 part Crème De Chocolate

Pour ingredients into a shaker with cracked ice and shake well. Strain into chilled martini glasses.

Rainbow Sherbet Martini

4 parts Orange Vodka
4 parts Raspberry Vodka
4 parts Peach Vodka
1 part Orange Liqueur
1 part Orange Juice
1 part Cranberry Juice

Pour ingredients into a shaker with cracked ice and shake well. Strain into chilled martini glasses. Garnish with an orange wedge.

Spiced Treat Martini

6 parts Cinnamon Vodka
1 part Chocolate Liqueur
1 part Coffee Liqueur

Pour ingredients into a shaker with cracked ice and shake well. Strain into chilled martini glasses. Garnish with a chocolate cocktail straw.

Sugar Plum

1 part Spiced Rum
1 part Plum Liqueur
1 part Crème de Noyeaux

Rim martini glasses with sugar and chill. Pour ingredients into a shaker with cracked ice and shake well. Strain into prepared martini glasses.

Sweet & Spicy Martini

6 parts Cinnamon Vodka
1 part Sweet Vermouth
1 part Triple Sec

Pour ingredients into a shaker with cracked ice and shake well. Strain into chilled martini glasses. Garnish with a cinnamon stick.

Sweet Hereafter

5 parts Vodka
2 parts Butterscotch Schnapps
1 part Peach Schnapps

Pour ingredients into a shaker with cracked ice and shake well. Strain into chilled martini glasses. Garnish with an orange twist.

The Bella Notte

1 part White Crème de Cacao
1 part Dark Crème de Cacao
1 part Hazelnut Liqueur
1 part Irish Cream
1 part cream

Swirl chocolate syrup in chilled martini glass. Pour ingredients into a shaker with cracked ice and shake well. Strain into chilled martini glasses.

The Weezer

6 parts Vodka
1 part Coffee Liqueur
1 part White Chocolate Liqueur
1 splash Raspberry Liqueur

Pour ingredients into a shaker with cracked ice and shake well. Strain into chilled martini glasses. Garnish with a Hershey's Kiss.

Tootsie Roll Martini

3 parts Vodka
1 part Crème de Cacao
2 parts Orange Juice

Pour ingredients into a shaker with cracked ice and shake well. Strain into chilled martini glasses. Garnish with an orange twist.

Tootsie Roll Martini 2

6 parts Vodka
1 part Chocolate Liqueur
1 part Grand Marnier

Pour ingredients into a shaker with cracked ice and shake well. Strain into chilled martini glasses. Garnish with an orange twist.

Truffle Martini

6 parts Strawberry Vodka
1 part Grand Marnier
1 part Chocolate Liqueur

Pour ingredients into a shaker with cracked ice and shake well. Strain into chilled martini glasses. Garnish with an orange twist.

Vanilla Cream Martini

16 parts Vanilla Vodka
1 part Sherry
1 part Irish Cream

Pour ingredients into a shaker with cracked ice and shake well. Strain into chilled martini glasses. Garnish with a vanilla bean.

What is That Martini?

6 parts Vodka
1 part Sambuca

Pour ingredients into a shaker with cracked ice and shake well. Strain into chilled martini glasses. Garnish with a licorice twist and 3 coffee beans.

Yahoo

1 part Vanilla Vodka
2 parts Chocolate Milk

Rim martini glasses with melted chocolate and place in freezer to harden chocolate. Pour ingredients into a shaker with cracked ice and shake well. Strain into prepared martini glasses. Garnish with shaved chocolate.

Z-tini

1 part Vodka
1 part Bailey's
1 part Raspberry Liqueur
1 part Strawberry Schnapps
1 part Cream

Pour ingredients into a shaker with cracked ice and shake well. Strain into chilled martini glasses.

Zinamon Appletini

8 parts Infused Vodka
1 part Amaretto

Infuse vodka with cinnamon and apple jolly ranchers. Pour ingredients into a shaker with cracked ice and shake well. Strain into chilled martini glasses.

THE MOCKTINIS

"Abstainer: a weak person who
yields to the temptation of
denying himself a pleasure."

— Ambrose Bierce —

Acapulco Gold

6 parts Pineapple Juice
2 parts Coconut Cream
2 parts Fresh Cream
1 part Grapefruit Juice

Pour all ingredients into a shaker with cracked ice and shake well. Pour into chilled martini glasses. Garnish with a pineapple wedge.

Anita-tini

3 parts Orange Juice
1 part Lemon Juice
1 splash Soda Water
2 dashes Bitters

Pour all ingredients except Soda into a shaker with cracked ice and shake well. Strain into chilled martini glasses. Add a splash of Soda to each glass. Garnish with fresh fruit.

Barley-tini

1 part Lemon Barley
1 part Lemonade
1 splash Lime Juice

Pour all ingredients into a shaker with cracked ice and shake well. Strain into chilled martini glasses. Garnish with a lemon twist.

Beach Blanket Bingo

1 part Cranberry Juice
1 part Grapefruit Juice
1 part Club Soda

Pour juices into a shaker with cracked ice and shake well. Strain into chilled martini glasses. Top with Club Soda. Garnish with an orange wedge.

Boo Boo's Special

2 parts Orange Juice
2 parts Pineapple Juice
1 splash Lemon Juice
1 dash Bitters
1 dash Grenadine Syrup

Pour all ingredients into a shaker with cracked ice and shake well. Strain into chilled martini glasses. Garnish with fresh fruit.

Capucinitini

1 part Peppermint Cordial
4 dashes Fresh Cream

Pour all ingredients into a shaker with cracked ice and shake well. Strain into chilled martini glasses. Garnish with shaved chocolate.

Cardinal Punchini

3 parts Cranberry Juice
1 part Gingerale
1 splash Orange Juice
1 dash Lemon Juice
1 dash Bar Sugar

Pour ingredients except Gingerale into a shaker with cracked ice and shake well. Strain into chilled martini glasses. Top with Gingerale. Garnish with fresh cranberries.

Cinderellatini

1 part Orange Juice
1 part Pineapple Juice
1 splash Sour Mix
1 splash Club Soda
1 dash Grenadine Syrup

Pour ingredients except Club Soda and Grenadine into a shaker with cracked ice and shake well. Strain into chilled martini glasses. Top with Club Soda and drizzle Grenadine in centre of drink. Garnish with a cherry.

Down East Delight

1 part Cranberry Juice
1 part Pineapple Juice
1 part Orange Juice
1 dash Bar Sugar

Pour ingredients into a shaker with cracked ice and shake well. Strain into chilled martini glasses. Garnish with a cherry.

Godchild

5 parts Lemonade
1 splash Lemon Juice
1 splash Syrop de Cassis

Pour ingredients except Syrop de Cassis into a shaker with cracked ice and shake well. Place a single ice cube into each chilled martini glass. Drizzle Syrop de Cassis over ice cube so that it pools in bottom of glass. Strain mixture in shaker slowly into prepared martini glasses. Garnish with a lemon slice.

Greciantini

4 parts Peach Juice
2 parts Orange Juice
1 part Lemon Juice
1 dash Soda Water

Pour ingredients except Soda into a shaker with cracked ice and shake well. Strain into chilled martini glasses. Top with Soda Water. Garnish with fresh fruit.

I'll Fake Manhattan

1 part Orange Juice
1 part Cranberry Juice
2 dashes Orange Bitters
1 dash Grenadine Syrup
1 dash Lemon Juice

Pour ingredients into a shaker with cracked ice and shake well. Strain into chilled martini glasses. Garnish with a lemon twist.

Jersey Lily

4 parts Carbonated Apple Juice
1 dash Bar Sugar
1 dash Bitters

Pour ingredients into a pitcher with cracked ice and stir gently. Pour into chilled martini glasses. Garnish with an apple wedge.

Jersey Lily 2

3 parts Apple Juice
1 part Lemon-Lime Soda
1 dash Bitters

Pour ingredients into a pitcher with cracked ice and stir gently. Pour into chilled martini glasses. Garnish with an apple wedge.

Lime Rickitini

3 parts Club Soda
1 part Lime Juice
1 part Bar Sugar
1 dash Bitters

Pour ingredients except Soda into a shaker with cracked ice and shake well. Strain into chilled martini glasses. Top with Club Soda. Garnish with a lime wedge.

Miami Vice

1 part Rootbeer
1 part Cream
1 splash Chocolate Syrup
1 splash Cola

Pour all ingredients except Cola into a shaker with cracked ice and shake well. Strain into chilled martini glasses. Top with Cola.

Mock Ceasartini

5 parts Clamato Juice
1 part Lemon Juice
1 splash Lime Juice
1 dash Worchestershire Sauce
1 dash Tabasco Sauce

Rim chilled martini glasses with celery salt. Pour all ingredients into a shaker with cracked ice and shake well. Strain into prepared martini glasses. Garnish with thin celery spears.

Mock Champagne-tini

2 parts Grapefruit Juice
1 part Orange Juice
1 splash Bar Sugar
1 splash Grenadine Syrup
1 splash Gingerale

Pour ingredients except Gingerale into a shaker with cracked ice and shake well. Strain into chilled martini glasses. Top with Gingerale.

Mock Champagne-tini 2

6 parts Lemon-Lime Soda
1 part Apple Juice
1 splash Lemon Juice

Pour ingredients into a pitcher with cracked ice and stir gently. Strain into chilled martini glasses. Garnish with a lemon twist.

Mock Daisy Crustatini

2 parts Fresh Lime Juice
1 splash Syrop de Framboise
1 splash Soda Water
1 dash Grenadine Syrup

Pour ingredients except Soda and Grenadine into a shaker with cracked ice and shake well. Strain into chilled martini glasses. Top with Soda Water. Drizzle Grenadine into each glass. Garnish with fresh raspberries and a sprig of fresh mint.

Mock Marguaritini

2 parts Sour Mix
1 splash Lime Juice
1 splash Orange Juice

Rim chilled martini glasses with coarse salt. Pour ingredients into a shaker with cracked ice and shake well. Strain into prepared martini glasses. Garnish with a lime wedge.

Mock Pina Coladatini

3 parts Pineapple Juice
2 parts Cream of Coconut

Pour all ingredients into a shaker with cracked ice and shake well. Strain into chilled martini glasses. Top with whipped cream, a cherry and a pineapple wedge.

Mock Sangriatini

2 parts Red Grape Juice
1 part Club Soda
1 splash Lime Juice
1 splash Orange Juice

Pour ingredients into a pitcher with cracked ice and stir gently. Strain into chilled martini glasses. Garnish with a pineapple slice and an orange slice.

Mock White Sangriatini

4 parts White Grape Juice
1 part Pink Grapefruit Juice
1 splash Lime Juice
1 splash Club Soda

Pour ingredients except Soda into a shaker with cracked ice and shake well. Strain into chilled martini glasses. Top with Club Soda. Garnish with a slice of pink grapefruit.

Montego Bay

1 part Orange Juice
1 part Sour Mix
1 splash Grenadine Syrup
1 splash Lemon-Lime Soda

Pour all ingredients except Soda into a shaker with cracked ice and shake well. Strain into chilled martini glasses. Top with Soda. Garnish with an orange slice.

Nicholas

1 part Grapefruit Juice
1 part Orange Juice
1 part Sour Mix
1 splash Grenadine Syrup

Pour all ingredients into a shaker with cracked ice and shake well. Strain into chilled martini glasses. Garnish with a cherry.

PMS

1 part Orange Juice
1 part Cranberry Juice
1 splash Soda

Pour all ingredients except Soda into a shaker with cracked ice and shake well. Strain into chilled martini glasses. Add a splash of soda to each glass.

Pac Man

2 parts Lemon
2 parts Gingerale Juice
1 dash Grenadine Syrup
1 dash Bitters

Pour all ingredients except Gingerale into a shaker with cracked ice and shake well. Strain into chilled martini glasses. Top with Gingerale. Garnish with an orange slice.

Pearls and Lace

1 part Orange Soda
1 part Cola
1 part Rootbeer
1 part Lemon-Lime Soda
1 splash Lemonade

Pour all ingredients into a shaker with cracked ice and stir gently. Pour into chilled martini glasses.

Pink Champagne

1 part Pink Grapefruit Juice
1 part Lemon Juice
1 dash Bitters
1 dash Lime Juice
1 dash Grenadine Syrup
1 splash Club Soda

Pour all ingredients except Soda into a shaker with cracked ice and shake well. Strain into chilled martini glasses. Top with Soda.

Pink Lemontini

3 parts Pink Lemonade
1 splash Syrop de Framboise
1 splash Lime Juice

Pour all ingredients into a shaker with cracked ice and shake well. Strain into chilled martini glasses. Garnish with a lemon slice.

Pony's Neck

5 parts Gingerale
2 dash Bitters
1 dash Lime Juice

Pour all ingredients into a pitcher with cracked ice and stir gentle. Strain into chilled martini glasses. Garnish with a lemon twist and a cherry.

Pussyfoot

1 part Orange Juice
1 part Lemon Juice
1 part Lime Juice
1 splash Soda Water

Pour all ingredients except Soda into a shaker with cracked ice and shake well. Strain into chilled martini glasses. Top with soda. Garnish with a cherry.

Rosie's Special Mocktini

1 part Tea
1 part Orange Juice
1 splash of Soda

Rim chilled martini glasses with sugar. Pour all ingredients except Soda into a shaker with cracked ice and shake well. Strain into prepared martini glasses. Top with Soda. Garnish with a cherry.

Rosy Pippintini

4 parts Apple Juice
1 part Gingerale
1 splash Grenadine Syrup
1 splash Sour Mix

Pour all ingredients except Gingerale into a shaker with cracked ice and shake well. Strain into chilled martini glasses. Top with Gingerale. Garnish with an apple slice.

San Francisco

1 part Pineapple Juice
1 part Orange Juice
1 part Grapefruit Juice
1 part Sour Mix
2 dashes of Grenadine Syrup
1 splash Soda

Pour all ingredients except Soda into a shaker with cracked ice and shake well. Strain into chilled martini glasses. Top with Soda.

Snow and Ice

2 parts Cream
1 part Sugar
1 splash Vanilla
1 part Snow (newly fallen)

Place a fresh snowball into each chilled martini glass. Pour all ingredients except snow into a shaker with cracked ice and shake well. Strain over snowballs in the martini glasses.

Snow and Ice 2

2 part Fruit Juice (your choice)
1 splash Lemon Juice
1 part Snow (newly fallen)

Rim chilled martini glasses with sugar. Place a fresh snowball into each glass. Pour all ingredients except Snow into a shaker with cracked ice and shake well. Strain over snowballs in the martini glasses.

Sonoma Nouveau

5 parts Alcohol Free White Wine
1 splash Soda
1 splash Cranberry Juice

Pour all ingredients except Soda into a shaker with cracked ice and shake well. Strain into chilled martini glasses. Top with Soda. Garnish with cranberries.

Summertime

1 part Orange Juice
1 part Lemon Juice
1 part Grapefruit Juice
1 splash Bar Sugar
1 part Vanilla Ice Cream
1 splash Soda Water

Place a small scoop of Vanilla Ice Cream into chilled martini glasses. Pour all remaining ingredients except Soda into a shaker with cracked ice and shake well. Pour over ice cream. Top with Soda. Garnish with an orange slice.

Sunset Cool-tini

8 parts Cranberry Juice
5 parts Orange Juice
1 splash Lemon Juice
1 splash Gingerale

Pour all ingredients except Gingerale into a shaker with cracked ice and shake well. Strain into chilled martini glasses. Add a splash of Gingerale to each glass. Garnish with an orange wedge.

Surfer's Paradise

3 parts Lemonade
1 part Lime Juice
3 dashes Bitters

Pour all ingredients into a shaker with cracked ice and shake well. Strain into chilled martini glasses. Garnish with an orange slice.

Tomato Cool-tini

5 parts Tomato Juice
1 splash Lemon Juice
1 splash Tonic Water

Rim chilled martini glasses with coarse salt. Pour all ingredients except Tonic into a shaker with cracked ice and shake well. Strain into prepared martini glasses. Add a splash of Tonic to each glass. Garnish with a lemon wedge.

Transfusion

1 part Grape Juice
2 parts Lemon-Lime Soda
1 splash Lime Juice

Pour all ingredients into a pitcher with cracked ice and stir gently. Strain into prepared martini glasses. Garnish with a lime wedge.

Transfusion 2

1 part White Grape Juice
2 parts Sparkling Non-alcoholic White Wine
1 splash Lime Juice

Pour all ingredients into a pitcher with cracked ice and stir gently. Strain into prepared martini glasses. Garnish with frozen green grapes.

Unfuzzy Naveltini

2 parts Orange Juice
1 part Peach or Nectarine Juice
1 splash Lemon-Lime Soda
1 dash Grenadine Syrup

Pour all ingredients except Soda into a shaker with cracked ice and shake well. Strain into chilled martini glasses. Add a splash of Soda to each glass. Garnish with a cherry.

LIQUEURS DEFINED

"Give strong drink unto him that is ready to perish,
and wine unto those that be of heavy hearts.
Let him drink, and forget his poverty, and
remember his misery no more."

— Proverbs 31: 6-7 —

A

Absinthe
A bitter liqueur flavoured with wormwood. It is green or yellow in colour and due to its toxicity it was banned in the early 1900's. A milder form is Pastis.

Alize
A fruity liqueur consisting of a blend of passion fruit and cognac.

Amaretto
Almond flavoured liqueur made from apricot pits.

Amalfi Lemon Liqueur
A strong, sweet, lemon flavoured Italian Liqueur made by infusing fresh lemon (Sfusato Amalfitano variety) peels.

Amarula Wild Fruit Cream
A light chocolate flavoured South African cream liqueur made from the fruit of the Marula tree.

Amer Picon Bitter
Orange flavoured French apéritif cordial made from quinine and spices.

Anisette
Licorice flavoured liqueur made with anise seed. It is available in a white or red variety.

B

Bailey's Original Irish Cream
A chocolate flavoured cream liqueur made from Irish whiskey, cream and chocolate.

Bäska Droppar (Bitter Drops)
A cinnamon scented bitter liqueur made with wormwood, Seville bitter and cinnamon.

Bénédictine
A unique sweet herbal liqueur. Created by Bénédictine monks in 1510 as a treatment for malaria. The secret recipe includes a cognac base blended with juniper, myrrh, angelica, cloves, cardamom, cinnamon, vanilla, tea and honey. It is amber in colour.

Bolivar
A coffee flavoured Canadian liqueur. It is brown in colour with a rich coffee aroma.

Bundaberg Royal Liqueur
A chocolate and coffee flavoured liqueur made with Bundy Rum and flavourings.

C

Calvados
A dry apple brandy. It is made in Calvados in the Normandy region of northern France.

Campari
A dry bitter-sweet Italian apéritif. It is an infusion of aromatic and bitter herbs and orange peel. It is garnet in colour.

Chambord (Liqueur Royale de France)
A very sweet berry flavoured liqueur made from small black raspberries (framboises), other fruits, herbs and honey. It is dark purple in colour.

Chartreuse (green)
An ancient herbal liqueur developed by the Carthusian monks in the early 1600's. It has only been commercially produced since 1848. It is pale green in colour and refreshing. It is made from a grape brandy base and flavoured with 130 herbs and plants. Its sweetness is balanced by the bitterness of the herbs. The green variety is 100 proof.

Chartreuse (yellow)
It is a sweeter and milder version than the green variety. It is about 86 proof and is yellow in colour.

Cherry Heering
A cherry flavoured liqueur. Made from the juice of fresh, ripe Danish cherries.

Cointreau
A strongly flavoured orange liqueur (best triple sec). A French liqueur made from brandy and sweet and bitter Mediterranean and tropical orange peels.

Coconut Creole Liqueur - Bols
A coconut flavoured liqueur. Strong scent and flavour of fresh coconut.

Crème de Bananes - Bols
A thinner, lightly banana flavoured crème liqueur. Made from artificial fruit flavour.

Crème de Cacao
A sweet chocolate liqueur. Made of cocoa beans, vanilla and spices. It is available in brown and white varieties. Some brands are more artificially flavoured than others.

Crème de Cassis
A rich fruity liqueur made of black currants grown in Dijon, France.

Crème de Framboise
Raspberry flavoured liqueur.

Crème de Menthe
A mint liqueur consisting of several varieties of mints including peppermint and spearmint. Available in gold, green and white varieties.

Crème de Noyeaux
A nutty-fruity flavoured liqueur made with apricot pits, peach pits and almonds.

Crème de Violette
An amethyst coloured Dutch liqueur. It is flavoured with the oil of violets and vanilla.

Curaçao
An orange flavoured triple sec liqueur. Flavoured with the dried peel form small green oranges grown in the Dutch West Indies. Available in blue, orange and clear varieties.

Cynar
An Italian apéritif. It is made with artichokes and is flavoured with quinine.

D

Drambuie
A traditional Scotch liqueur made on the Isle of Skye. "An Dram Buidheach", the drink that satisfies. Scotch whiskey flavoured with heather honey and spices, not very sweet.

E

Elixir de Spa
A sweet herb liqueur from Belgium. Similar to Jägermeister and fairly thick.

F

Frangelico Liqueur
A hazelnut flavoured Italian liqueur. Made of hazelnuts, vanilla and other flowers.

G

Galliano Liqueur
An herbal Italian liqueur, named for a famous war hero of 1896. It is made of anise and vanilla and 40 other herbs, berries, roots and flowers. It is bright yellow in colour.

Glayva
A strong, sweet honey and herb Scottish liqueur. Similar to Drambuie but much sweeter.

Godet
A Belgium white chocolate liqueur. It has a brandy base and is very tasty. Milky in colour.

Godiva Liqueur
A rich dark chocolate liqueur. A velvety Belgium liqueur. Dark brown in colour.

Godiva Cappuccino Liqueur
A chocolate, cappuccino flavoured Belgium liqueur. Medium brown in colour.

Godiva White Chocolate Liqueur.
A smooth white chocolate Belgium liqueur. White in colour.

Goldschläger
A Swiss cinnamon schnapps liqueur with gold leaf flakes floating in it. It is completely clear except for the gold leaf.

Goldwasser
A clear herb flavoured liqueur. It is made with orange zest, herbs and spices with the flavour of aniseed and caraway. It has flecks of gold leaf floating in it. It was originally made by Danziger. Some claim that it is the oldest known liqueur.

Grand Marnier
An orange flavoured French liqueur. A cognac base flavoured with the peels of bitter wild oranges.

H

Heather Cream Liqueur
A scotch whiskey and cream liqueur. It is sweetened with heather honey.

I

Irish Mist
An herb and honey liqueur. It is made with a whiskey base and flavoured with various herbs and sweetened with honey.

J

Jägermeister
A German herbal liqueur. A dark, very herbal flavoured blend of 56 roots, herbs and berries.

K

Kahlua
A classic coffee flavoured liqueur from Mexico.

Kirsch
A white brandy distilled from cherries and usually aged in a paraffin lined cask to prevent it from taking on the color of the wood. It is also known as cherry schnapps.

Koskenkorva Salmiakka
A licorice flavoured liqueur from Finland. It is flavoured with real licorice and not anise seed. Strong taste, not overly sweet, and thin. Black in colour.

Krupnikas
A honey vodka from Lithuania. It is thick and syrupy with a sweet, mild herbal flavour.

Kummel
A liqueur flavoured with caraway, anise seed and other herbs.

L

La Grande Passion
A passion fruit flavoured liqueur. It is made with Armagnac brandy. La Grande Passion is manufactured by the same French company that creates Grand Marnier.

Lemoncella
A spirit made by infusing lemon juice and peels with a base grain alcohol. It is yellow in colour.

Licor 43
A Spanish liqueur with a citrus and vanilla flavour. The recipe originated around 200 BC. It has 43 basic elements which are mainly fruits and herbs. It is also called Cuarenta Y Tres. It is bright yellow in colour.

Liquore Strega
A rich and spicy Italian liqueur. Legend has it that this was originally an aphrodisiac love potion. Strega is Italian for witch. It has a distinct clove and citrus flavour with a touch of bitterness. It is golden in colour.

Lochan Ora
A golden Scotch based liqueur. Its flavour is drawn from Curacao and Ceylon.

M

Malibu
A white rum based coconut flavoured liqueur. This Canadian liqueur is clear and sweet.

Mandarin Napoleon
A Belgium liqueur with the flavour of ripe tangerines. A cognac base flavoured with the peels of Andulsian tangerines. It is amber in colour.

Maraschino Liqueur
A cherry flavoured liqueur. It is made with Maraska cherries grown in Dalmatia in the former Yugoslavia. The cherries are sour.

Metaxa
A Greek liqueur made with a grape base. Brandy-like and slightly sweet.

Mezcal or Mescal
A spirit made from the distillation of the cactus (maguey or agave) and produced in small quantities in Mexico. It is distilled like tequila.

Midori
A sweet honeydew melon flavoured liqueur. It is made in Japan and is green in colour.

O

Ojen
A Spanish liqueur flavoured with anise.

Opal Nera

An Italian liqueur with the flavour and colour of black jellybeans. It is made with anise and elderflower with a hint of lemon. It is the colour of black opal.

Ouzo

A licorice flavoured liqueur from Greece.

P

Parfait Amour

A light purple coloured liqueur. It is made in France and is flavoured with rose petals, vanilla and almonds.

Pernod

An anise flavoured liqueur. It is yellow-green in colour and turns opalescent green and white when mixed with water and ice.

Pisa Nut Liqueur

An Italian almond flavoured liqueur. It tastes like marzipan. It is medium gold in colour and syrupy.

Polmos Old Krupnik Honey Vodka

A honey vodka from Poland made from a recipe dating back to the 1700's. It is sweet with an herbal flavour.

S

Sabra

A chocolate orange liqueur from Israel. It is a blend of Jaffa oranges and chocolate.

Sambuca

An Italian licorice flavoured liqueur. It is made from wild elderflowers, known as Witch elder, and licorice. It is sometimes flavoured with sweet anise and can be found in many varieties.

Slivovitz

A plum brandy made in Serbia.

Sloe Gin

A liqueur made from the fruit of sloeberry. It tastes somewhat like wild cherries and is red in colour.

Southern Comfort

An American peach flavoured liqueur. Made with a bourbon base it is sweet and amber in colour.

T

Tia Maria

A classic coffee flavoured liqueur from Jamaica. It is dark brown in colour.

Triple Sec

An orange flavoured liqueur. Made from Dutch West Indies orange peel. Rather like Curaçao but sweeter and higher proof. It is clear.

Truffles

A rich chocolate liqueur.

Tuaca

An orange flavoured liqueur. It is from Italy and has a hint of vanilla to its flavour.

W

Wild Turkey Liqueur

A spicy bourbon based liqueur from America. It is made from fully aged bourbon, herbs and spices. It is amber in colour.

Z

Zubrowka

A brand of buffalo grass vodka. It is made in Poland and Hungary and is yellow in colour. Each bottle contains a blade of buffalo grass. It is also known as Zubrowka Grass.

*"Always do sober what you said you'd do drunk.
That will teach you to keep your mouth shut."*

— Ernest Hemmingway —

OTHER INGREDIENTS

"Drink to me."

— Pablo Picasso —
His last Words

Apéritif
A wine taken before a meal to induce digestion.

Bar Sugar
A liquid sweetener. It can be made by dissolving sugar in hot water. It can also be purchased pre-made. It is used to sweeten sour or bitter cocktails.

Bitters
A bitter or bittersweet type of spirit made from different herbs, roots and plants. Bitters are used to flavour and add a dry zest to cocktails and cooking. They function as digestive aids and appetite stimulants. They are often used in before and after dinner cocktails.

Fino Sherry
The driest variety of sherry.

Grenadine (Grenadine Syrup)
A blood-red, strong syrup made from pomegranates. It is used for sweetening and to give cocktails a red color.

Lillet
A light, medium dry French apéritif. It is either red or white. It has a Bourdeax wine base which is flavoured with herbs, spices and fruits fortified with French Brandy.

Lime Cordial
A non-alcoholic lime syrup. It is a mixture of concentrated lime juice and sugar.

Orgeat Syrup
A bitter almond flavoured syrup.

Punt e Mes
A red vermouth made by Branca Products.

Sour Mix
A mixture of lemon juice and sugar syrup. Also called Sweet and Sour Mix or Bar Mix. It can be bought as a commercial brand or you can make your own.

Vermouth
Wine infused with herbs, alcohol, sugar, caramel and water according to specific recipes in Italy and France.

The two common types of Vermouth:

- Dry vermouth is white. It is used as an apéritif and is an essential part of the dry Martini.

- Sweet vermouth is white (bianco) or red (rosso). It is also used as an apéritif as well as in slightly sweet cocktails.

*"You're not drunk if you can lie on the floor
without holding on."*

— Dean Martin —

NAMES INDEXED

"The only green vegetables
I get are Martini Olives."

— B. F. Pierce —
M*A*S*H

I

J

K

L

R-E-M-O-R-S-E!

Those dry Martinis did the work for me;
Last night at twelve I felt immense,
Today I feel like thirty cents.
My eyes are bleared, my coppers hot,
I'll try to eat, but I cannot.
It is no time for mirth and laughter,
The cold, gray dawn of the morning after.

— George Ade —

INGREDIENTS INDEXED

"I drink when I have occasion, and sometimes when I have no occasion."

— Miguel De Cervantes —

How to use this index:

Only the ingredients of the Martinis are in this index. The ingredients in the Mocktinis are not indexed. If the ingredient is not a contributing portion of the recipe (1 part or greater), it is not indexed.

After each entry in this index you will see a list of hyphenated numbers separated by commas. The first portion of the hyphenated number indicates the page on which the recipe is located and the number following the hyphen indicates the sequence in which the recipe occurs. eg: 121-3 indicates 3rd recipe on page 121.

A

Absinthe: 85-3

Alize: 57-3, 73-1, 80-3, 118-6

Almond Liqueur: 39-1, 121-6

Amaretto: 24-4, 27-2, 85-1, 95-2, 96-4, 107-6, 108-4, 123-3, 123-4, 132-3, 143-4, 145-4, 145-5, 151-1, 151-2, 151-3, 156-2

Anise Liqueur: 105-2, 115-5, 149-4

Anisette: 105-2, 149-4

Apple Cider: 62-4

Apple Liqueur: 69-5

Apple Schnapps: 62-5

Apricot Nectar: 66-4

Aquivit: 40-5

B

Bailey's: 41-6, 43-1, 95-2, 105-1, 133-3, 133-4, 137-2, 142-4, 143-4, 145-3, 152-2, 156-1

Banana Liqueur: 30-4, 39-1, 39-5, 40-1, 59-2, 63-5, 79-1, 79-5, 115-2, 138-3, 143-2

Beer: 90-6, 118-2

Bénédictine: 27-4, 28-3

Black Currant Schnapps: 19-5

Black Currant Liqueur: 67-4

Blackberry Liqueur: 27-6

Blueberry Schnapps: 35-5, 60-4

211

F